First World War
and Army of Occupation
War Diary
France, Belgium and Germany

30 DIVISION
Divisional Troops
Prince of Wales's Volunteers (South Lancashire Regiment)
11th Battalion Pioneers
6 November 1915 - 27 May 1918

WO95/2323/3

The Naval & Military Press Ltd
www.nmarchive.com
Published in association with The National Archives

Published by

The Naval & Military Press Ltd

Unit 10 Ridgewood Industrial Park,
Uckfield, East Sussex,
TN22 5QE England
Tel: +44 (0) 1825 749494

www.naval-military-press.com

www.nmarchive.com

This diary has been reprinted in facsimile from the original. Any imperfections are inevitably reproduced and the quality may fall short of modern type and cartographic standards.

© **Crown Copyright**
Images reproduced by permission of The National Archives, London, England, 2015.

Contents

Document type	Place/Title	Date From	Date To
Heading	WO95/2323/3 11th Bn 5th Lancs Regt Nov 1915-May 1918 Oct 1918-June 1919		
Heading	30th Division Divl Troops 11th Bn 5th Lancs Regt (Pioneers) Nov 1915-May 1918 Oct 1918 To June 1919 To UK in Interim Period		
Heading	(Attached) 25 Divisional Troops 11 Bn South Lancashire Regiment (Pioneer) 1918 Oct-1919 June		
Heading	11th Bn. South Lancashire Regiment. (Pioneers) War Diary for the month of 6th October 1918-31st October, 1918. Vol 25		
War Diary	Le Havre	07/10/1918	13/10/1918
Miscellaneous	11th Bn. South Lancashire Regiment. (Pioneers).	01/11/1918	01/11/1918
Heading	11th Bn. South Lancashire Regiment. (Pioneers). War Diary for the month of 1st November, 1918 to 30th November, 1918. V. 32		
Miscellaneous	D.A.G. 3rd. Echelon.	03/04/1919	03/04/1919
War Diary		10/11/1918	10/11/1918
War Diary	Maroiles	11/11/1918	29/11/1918
Miscellaneous	11th Bn. South Lancashire Regiment. (Pioneers).	01/11/1919	01/11/1919
War Diary		01/12/1918	19/12/1918
War Diary		18/12/1918	13/01/1919
War Diary		01/02/1919	28/02/1919
War Diary		01/03/1919	31/03/1919
War Diary		22/03/1919	31/03/1919
War Diary		06/06/1919	13/06/1919
War Diary		01/04/1919	30/04/1919
War Diary		01/05/1919	31/05/1919
War Diary		17/05/1919	31/05/1919
Heading	30th Division Nov 15 May 18 V.1		
Heading	Volume 1 November 1915 War Diary Of 11th (S) Bn S. Lancashire Regt (S. Helens Pioneers).		
War Diary	Larkhill Camp.	06/11/1915	06/11/1915
War Diary	S'hampton	06/11/1915	06/11/1915
War Diary	Havre	06/11/1915	07/11/1915
War Diary	Pont Remy	08/11/1915	08/11/1915
War Diary	Bussus	08/11/1915	08/11/1915
War Diary	Bussuel	08/11/1915	17/11/1915
War Diary	Flesselles	17/11/1915	17/11/1915
War Diary	Berneuil	28/11/1915	28/11/1915
Heading	30th Division 11th S. Lancs Vol:2 Decr 15		
Heading	Volume 21. December 1915 11th (S) Bn S. Lancs Regt (Pioneers) War Diary For December 1915. 31st Decr 1915 H Harrington Lt. Colonel Comdg 11th (S) Bn. S. Lanc Regt (Pioneers)		
War Diary	Flesselles	26/11/1915	26/11/1915
War Diary	Mailly Maillet	28/11/1915	31/12/1915
Heading	11th S. Lancs Vol 3		
War Diary		01/01/1916	01/01/1916
War Diary	Pernois	05/01/1916	14/01/1916
War Diary	Froissy	21/01/1916	28/01/1916

Type	Description	Date From	Date To
War Diary	Suzanne	28/01/1916	28/01/1916
War Diary	Bray	30/01/1916	31/01/1916
Heading	11th S. Lancs Vol:4		
Heading	War Diary Of 11th (S) Bn S Lancs Regt (Pioneers) 1st Feb 1916 to 29th Feby 1916 Volume 4 H Harrington Lt Colonel Comg 11th S Lancs Regt (Pioneers) 29/2/16 Volume 4		
War Diary	Bray	03/02/1916	29/02/1916
Heading	War Diary 11th (S) Bn S. Lancs Regt (Pioneers) for Month of March 1916 Volume No: 5 11 S Lancs Vol 5		
War Diary	Suzanne	01/03/1916	01/03/1916
War Diary	Bray	10/03/1916	10/03/1916
War Diary	Suzanne	11/03/1916	16/03/1916
War Diary	Meaulte	19/03/1916	31/03/1916
Heading	War Diary of 11th S Lancs Regt. (Pioneers) Vol No. 6 April 1916 11th South Lancs Vol 6		
War Diary		31/03/1916	22/04/1916
Heading	War Diary of The 11th (S) Bn South Lancs Regt. (Pioneers) 1st May 1916 to 31st May 1916 (Volume 7) 11 S Lancs Vol 7		
War Diary	Vaux En-Amienois	02/05/1916	03/05/1916
War Diary	Corbie	04/05/1916	31/05/1916
War Diary		16/05/1916	26/05/1916
Heading	War Diary of 11th (S) Bn. South Lancashire Regiment. (Pioneers) From 1st June 1916 to 31st June 1916. (Volume No 8). 11 S Lancs Vol 8		
War Diary		01/06/1916	01/06/1916
War Diary		31/05/1916	31/05/1916
War Diary		03/06/1916	15/06/1916
War Diary		11/06/1916	30/06/1916
Heading	11 S Lancs July 1916		
Heading	War Diary of 11th Bn. South Lancashire Regiment. (Pioneers) from 1st July 1916 to 31st July, 1916. Volume 9		
War Diary		30/07/1916	30/07/1916
War Diary		01/07/1916	22/07/1916
Miscellaneous	11th (S) Bn. South Lancashire Regt. (Pioneers).	31/07/1916	31/07/1916
Map	Trenches & Dug By 11th S Lancs Regt once Offensive of 1.7.16		
Map	Those Marked over in Blacks Dug by 11th S Lancs Regt. on 1st-3rd July 1916		
Heading	30th Divisional Pioneers 1/11th Battalion South Lancashire Regiment August 1916		
War Diary		01/08/1916	28/08/1916
War Diary		24/08/1916	24/08/1916
Heading	War Diary of 11th (S) Bn. South Lancashire Regt. From 1st Septr. 1916 to 30th Septr 1916 (Volume No 11)		
War Diary		01/09/1916	28/09/1916
Heading	War Diary of 11th (S) Battn. South Lancashire Regt. (Pioneers) from October 1st, 1916 to 31st October, 1916 Volume 12		
War Diary		01/10/1916	25/10/1916
Heading	War Diary of 11th (S) Bn. South Lancashire Regiment. (Pioneers). from 1st November, 1916 to 30th November, 1916. Volume 13		
War Diary		06/11/1916	10/11/1916

Heading	11th (S) Bn. South Lancashire Regt. (Pioneers). War Diary of the 11th (S) Bn. S. Lancs. Regt. (Pioneers). 1st Decr. 1916. to 31st Decr. 1916. Volume No. 14		
Heading	From O.C. 11th S Lancs Regt (Pioneers)		
War Diary		01/12/1916	25/12/1916
Heading	11th (S) Bn. South Lancashire Regt. (Pioneers). War Diary of the 11th (S) Bn. South Lancashire Regt. (Pioneers) 1st January, 1917 to 31st January, 1917. Volume No. 15		
War Diary	In the Field Berles-au-Bois	08/01/1917	22/01/1917
Heading	11th (S) Bn. South Lancashire Regt. (Pioneers). War Diary of the 11th (S) Bn. South Lancashire Regt. (Pioneers). 1st February, 1917 to 28th February, 1917. Volume 16		
War Diary	Lucheux	01/03/1917	27/03/1917
Heading	War Diary of 11th (S) Battn. South Lancashire Regt. (Pioneers) from 1st March, 1917 to 31st March, 1917. Volume No 17		
War Diary		18/03/1917	22/03/1917
Heading	11th (S) Bn. South Lancashire Regt. (Pioneers). War Diary of the 11th (S) Bn. South Lancashire Regiment. (Pioneers). from 1st April, 1917 to 30th April, 1917 (Volume No. 18).		
War Diary	Blairville	01/04/1917	28/04/1917
Heading	11th (S) Battn. South Lancashire Regt. (Pioneers). War Diary of the 11th (S) Bn. Lancashire Regt. (Pioneers). From 1st May, 1917 to 31st May, 1917. (Volume 19)		
War Diary			
Heading	11th (S) Battn. South Lancashire Regt. (Pioneers). War Diary of 11th (S) Bn. South Lancashire Regt. (Pioneers). From 1st June. 1917 to 30th June, 1917. Volume 21		
War Diary	Ypres	00/06/1917	00/06/1917
Heading	War Diary of the 11th (S) Bn. South Lancashire Regiment. (Pioneers). 1st July, 1917 to 31st July, 1917. (Volume No. 22.)		
War Diary		01/07/1917	31/07/1917
Miscellaneous	11th (S) Bn. South Lancashire Regt. (Pioneers). Work of the Battalion on Zero Day (31st July, 1917).	31/07/1917	31/07/1917
Heading	War Diary of the 11th (S) Bn. S. Lancashire Regt. (Pioneers). from 1st August, 1917 to 31st August, 1917 Volume No. 23		
War Diary	In the Field.	00/08/1917	00/08/1917
Heading	War Diary of 11th (S) Bn. South Lancashire Regt., (Pioneers). from 1st September to 30th Sept. 1917 Volume 24		
War Diary	In the Field.	00/09/1917	00/09/1917
Heading	War Diary of 11th (S) Battn. South Lancashire Regt. (Pioneers) from 1st October, 1917 to 31st October, 1917. (Volume 25.)		
War Diary	Spy Farm Nr. Kemmel.	00/10/1917	00/10/1917
Map			
Heading	War Diary of the 11th (S) Bn. South Lancashire Regiment. (Pioneers). from 1st November, 1917 to 30th November, 1917. (Volume No. 26).		
War Diary	Spy Farm	01/11/1917	01/11/1917

Heading	War Diary of the 11th (S) Bn. South Lancashire Regt. (Pioneers). 1st December, 1917 to 31st December, 1917 Vol 26		
War Diary	Zillebeke Bund.	01/12/1917	01/12/1917
Heading	War Diary of 11th (S) Battalion, South Lancashire Regt., (Pioneers). from 1st January, 1918 to 31st January, 1918 (Volume 28.)		
War Diary		31/01/1918	31/01/1918
Heading	War Diary of 11th (S) Bn. South Lancashire Regt. (Pioneers). from 1st February 1918 to 28th February 1918. Volume 29		
War Diary		01/02/1918	28/02/1918
Heading	Pioneers. 30th Div. War Diary 11th Battn. The South Lancashire Regiment. March 1918		
Heading	War Diary of 11th (S) Bn. South Lancashire Regt., (Pioneers). from 1st March 1918 to 31st March 1918. Volume 30		
War Diary		01/03/1918	30/03/1918
Miscellaneous	11th. South Lancashire Regt. (Pioneers). Report on Operation From 21st to 28th. March 1918 Inclusive.	02/04/1918	02/04/1918
Heading	War Diary of 11th (S) Bn. South Lancashire Regt., (Pioneers). From 1st April, 1918 to 30th April, 1918. Volume 31		
War Diary	Lanchieres	31/03/1918	30/04/1918
Heading	War Diary of 11th (S) Bn. South Lancashire Regt., (Pioneers). from 1st May, 1918 to 31st May, 1918. Volume 32		
War Diary	L.23.c.9.9. (Sheet 27)	01/05/1918	27/05/1918

WO 95/ 2323/3

11th Bn 5th Lancs Regt

Nov 1915 — May 1918

Oct 1918 — June 1919

30TH DIVISION
DIVL TROOPS

11TH BN 8TH LANCS REGT
(PIONEERS)
NOV 1915 - MAY 1918

α OCT 1918 TO JUNE 1919

(To UK IN INTERIM PERIOD)

(ATTACHED) 25 DIVISIONAL TROOPS

11 BN South Lancashire Regiment (Pioneer)
1918 OCT - 1919 JUNE

11th Bn. South Lancashire Regiment. (Pioneers). 25 DIV

WAR DIARY

for

the month

of

6th OCTOBER 1918 — 31st OCTOBER, 1918.

....

WAR DIARY
or
INTELLIGENCE SUMMARY.
(Erase heading not required.)

Army Form C. 2118.

Place	Date	Hour	Summary of Events and Information	Remarks and references to Appendices
Le Havre	4/10/18		½ Bn arrived at Le Havre from Aldershot Area	
	8/10/18		Remainder arrived at Le Havre from Aldershot Area. The Battalion on arrival from England was composed largely of "B" men & a total of 36 Officers. Marched up to No 1 Rest Camp Le Havre & stayed there	
	10/10/18		until the 10th Oct 1918 in the meantime all ranks were being fitted up with deficiencies in clothing & equipment prior to proceeding up the line.	
	11/10/18		Bn arrived by train at ROISEL Railhead & remained under canvas there for the night, moving following day the	
	12/10/18		12th Oct 1918 by march route for ESTRÉE Mayring [?] here the night & proceeding on 13th Oct 1918 by march route to	
	13/10/18		PREMONT. On the 11th Oct's 1918 the Battn came under the orders of the 25th Divn & which we were to be brigaded. The attached is copy of brief narrative of part taken by Battn in Operations from 13th Oct to 31st Oct 1918.	

11th Bn. South Lancashire Regiment. (Pioneers).

Brief Narrative of part taken by the Battalion in operations etc. since arrival with 25th Division to 31/10/18.

13/10/18. 14/10/18.	The Battalion joined the 25th Division on the 13/10/18 and went into Billets at PREMONT. On the 14/10/18 work was carried out by all 3 Coys on Roads in the PREMONT – SERRIN – ELINCOURT Area under the C.R.E. 25th Division.
15/10/18.	On the 15th inst work was continued on Roads in the above area which consisted of the filling in of shell holes, craters, and drainage. On the 16/10/18 orders were received to move the Battalion to
16/10/18.	forward area ; the assembly of Battalion was as under to 2 Coys in Railway Cutting South of MOUROIS and 1 Coy at P.17.a.central. East of REUMONT. preparatory to work in connection with operations by XIII Corps on Le CATEAU Sector on 17/10/18.
17/10/18.	1 N.C.O. & 40 men worked on the Bridging Park under C.E. Corps for purpose of loading Lorries. Remainder of Company standing to waiting orders. Later the party on the Bridging park was increased to half Company. 1 Company worked in reliefs on Railway Bridge, clearing road at Q.15.b.4.1. Work on this job was carried on overnight in half Company reliefs. 2 Coys under orders of C.E. Corps carried out work on clearing of the MARETZ – LE CATEAU Road. Half Coy working on Bridge No 1 Le Cateau with R.E.s.
18/10/18.	Headquarters Details moved to Billets at HONNECHY. 1 Coy worked on clearing of debris at Railway Bridge, also cleared Road Le Cateau from K.34.a.6.2. to Bridge No 1 after which they joined B.H.Q. in Billets at HONNECHY. 1 Coy still located at Bridging Park. Half Coy of which worked on Bridge No.1. at Le CATEAU.
19/10/18.	Battalion moved from HONNECHY to ST. BENIN. The party working at the Bridging Park and on Bridge No 1 were relieved in the afternoon by the Sussex Pioneer Bn. After relief the party joined us at ST BENIN. 1 Company proceeded to work on following roads in 8 hour reliefs commencing at 19.00 hours. (i) Q.22.a.6.4. – Q.4.b.5.0. (ii) Q.4.b.5.0. – Q.17.d. (iii) Q.4.b.5.0. – K.34.d. thence South to Q.18.d.8.4. (iv) Q.18.d.8.4. – BAZUEL. The adjoining roads were also reconnoitred and reports forwarded to the C.R.E. 25th Division. The above Company was relieved and work continued on the same roads up to 13.00 hours 20/10/18.
20/10/18.	Relief again took place by a further Company at 13.00 hours, but the majority of the labour was concentrated on Q.14.b.5.0. Southwards to Q.17.d. Orders received to work on fallen bridge at Q.4.d.5.0. This work was very important and half Company reliefs were carried out night and day commencing at 17.00 hours in 4 hour shifts.
21/10/18.	On the 21st work was still being carried on by reliefs. 1 Company assisting the 182 Tunnelling Coy R.E. on the Plank Road Deviation in Q.5.c.
22/10/18.	Work still continued on the above Bridge and Plank deviation.
23/10/18.	In connection with operations to be carried out by the 3rd & 4th Armies, the following work was allotted to the Battalion. 1 Coy to clear Block at Railway Bridge at R.1.d.0.4. so that road from K.35.d.6.0. to R.8.b.6.5. BAZUEL was practicable for all Transport.

sheet 2.

23/10/18 (contd) 1 Coy on road from K.35.d.6.0. to POMMEREUIL Road to be opened for all traffic, including 6" Guns Mk VII.

1 Coy to open road from BAZUEL through R.3.a.central to POMMEREUIL and also ensure the road from Q.18.a.9.4. through BAZUEL kept open for all traffic.
All forward roads were reconnoitred closely behind the Advance and work carried out immediately on the roads as far as the advance would permit.
Roads detailed and worked upon as far as possible.

(i) K.35.d.6.0. - BAZUEL at R.8.a.9.5.
(ii) L.20.b.2.0. - G.2.c.4.0.
(iii) L.16.b.5.3. - G.13.b.9.3.
(iv) L.26.d.9.4. - L.20.b.2.0.
(v) L.26.d.9.4. - L.29.a.4.4.

The whole of the roads detailed above were worked upon as far as Advance permitted, and kept open for all traffic during the day. Reports were prepared by Reconnoitring parties and forwarded to the C.R.E. 25th Division.

24/10/18. 1 Company worked on Forward roads.
1 Compaby worked on Fallen girder bridge at R.1.d.0.4. in half Coy reliefs.
1 Coy remained in Camp in Reserve. This Company relieved the Company working on the Fallen Girder Bridge in the evening

25/10/18 and 26/10/18. Work on the above carried out.
Headquarters moved from ST BENIN to LE CATEAU, 2 Coys joining us there after work that day, on Defensive Support Positions.
1 Company located at R.1.d.0.2.
2 Coys worked on Defensive Support Line which was prepared and taped out by the C.R.E.
G.1.d. central - G.1.d.8.4. G.2.c.0.3 - G.2.c.1.0. - G.8.a.2.7 thence along contour crossing the road from FONTAINE to G.15.b. a few yards S.E. of the Red Tree, thence to about G.7.c.3.5.

27/10/18. 1 Company employed on clearing of Block at R.1.d.0.4.
2 Coys employed on Defensive Support Positions.

28/10/18. The Defensive Support Position was amended and taped out by the Commanding Officer New line taped out was from Road at G.8.a.3.7. via G.8.a.5.4. & G.8.a.4.0. across road to G.8.c.3.9
2 Coys employed on the above Defensive Support Position.
1 Coy on clearing of Block at R.1.d.0.4.

29/10/18. Work as above carried out.

30/10/18. 1 Coy clearing road at R.1.d.0.4. forward.

1 Coy repairing road L.16.central - L.29.a. and L.24.a.0.0. cleaning of roads from Q.4.d.6.0. to Q.4.b.5.0. and the road from K.35.d.6.0. to L.29.a.
1 Company completing work in hand on the Defensive Support Positions.
After work, one Company changed billets and moved to HONNECHY preparatory to being employed in Operations to be undertaken at a later date.

31/10/18. 1 Coy working on Bridging at R.1.d.0.4. which opened for all traffic
1 Coy working on Forward Roads. 1 Coy located at HONNECHY (Training).

Dispositions of the Battalion on the 31/10/18.
Bn. Hd. Qrs. Transport and 1 Company at ST.BENIN.
1 Company at R.1.d.0.4.   1 Company at HONNECHY.
Sheet 57 B used for all Map references.
Casualties incurred.
2nd Lieut. R. CARR. } missing 23/10/18 whilst reconnoitring
32574 L.C. LORD S   }   forward roads last seen 6 pm 23/10/18

sheet 3.

Lieut. H.V. Worrall wounded 26/10/18.

9 O.Rs wounded and 1 O.R. Wounded (Gas) during period under review.

C. Champion Lieut.Colonel.

1/11/18.   Cdg.11th Bn. South Lancashire Regt (Pioneers).

11th Bn. South Lancashire Regiment. (Pioneers).

WAR DIARY

for

the month of

1st NOVEMBER, 1918 to 30th NOVEMBER, 1918.

D. A. G.
     3rd. ECHELON.

Herewith A.F.C. 2118 (War Diary) for the month of March 1919.
Kindly acknowledge receipt.

                                                Capt. & Adjt.
for O.C. 11th. Bn. South Lancashire Regiment (P).

11TH (S) BATTALION,
SOUTH LANCS.
REGT. (PIONEERS).

3/4/1919
Date

Army Form C. 2118.

WAR DIARY
or
INTELLIGENCE SUMMARY.
(Erase heading not required.)

Place	Date	Hour	Summary of Events and Information	Remarks and references to Appendices
	10/11/18		Battalion employed on the clearing, filling in of Craters &c in the vicinity of Landrecies - Maroilles.	
MAROILLES	11/11/18		Battalion moved to Bieets at SARS-POTERIES. At 07.30 hrs on 11/11/18 wire was received that hostilities would cease at 11-30 hrs that day.	
	12/11/18		Bn employed on work filling in of Craters in vicinity of SARS POTERIES	
	13/11/18		B.H.Q. + B Coy moved to vicinity of AVESNES where 'C' Coy had moved to on the 12/4/18.	
	18/11/18		Battn entered by march route moving C.R.S. playing the right 18/19 at TRSNIERES a moving C.R.S. 19th Nov 1918	
	20/11/18		Battn employed on Salving, clearing of devastated area in the vicinity of CRS, BAZUEL + POMMEREUIL	
	28/11/18		Continued work on Salving, clearing of areas moved to	
	29/11/18		QUIEVY by march route on 29/11/18 + continued on clearing + clearing of Bieets occupied by Battn	

11th Bn. South Lancashire Regiment.(Pioneers).

Brief Narrative of part taken by the Battalion in
operations since 23/10/18

23/10/18. In connection with operations to be carried out by the 3rd & 4th Armies, the following work was allotted to the Battalion.
1 Coy to clear Block at Railway Bridge at R.1.d.0.4. so that road from K.35.d.6.0 to R.8.b.6.5. BAZUEL was practicable for all Transport.

1 Coy to widen on road from K.35.d.6.0. to POMMEREUIL. Road to be opened for all Traffic, including 6" Guns Mk.VII

1 Coy to open road from BAZUEL through R.3.a.central to POMMEREUIL and also ensure the road from Q.18.a.9.4 through BAZUEL kept open for all traffic.

All forward roads were reconnoitred closely behind the Advance and work carried out immediately on the roads as far as the advance would permit.
Roads detailed and worked upon as far as possible :
(i)   K.35.d.6.0 – BAZUEL at R.8.a.9.5.
(ii) L.20.b.2.0. – G.2.c.4.0.
(iii) L.16.b.5.3. – G/13.b.9.7.
(iv) L.26.d.9.4. – L.20.b.2.0.
(v)   L.26.d.9.4. – L.29.a.4.4.

The whole of the roads detailed above were worked upon as far as Advance permitted, and kept open for all traffic during the day. Reports were prepared by reconnoitring parties and forwarded to the C.R.E. Division.

24/10/18. 1 Coy worked on Forward roads.
1 Coy worked on Fallen girder bridge at R.1.d.0.4. in half Coy reliefs.
1 Coy remained in Camp in Reserve. This Company relieved the Company working on the Fallen Girder Bridge in the evening.

25/10/18 & Work on the above carried out.
26/10/18. Headquarters moved from ST.BENIN to LE CATEAU. 2 Coys joining us there after work that day on Defensive Support Positions.
1 Company located at R.1.d.0.2.

26/10/18. 2 Coys worked on Defensive Support Line which was prepared and taped out by the C.R.E.
G.1.d.central – G.1.d.8.4 – G.2.c.0.3. – G.2.c.1.0. – G.8.a.2.7. thence along contour crossing the road from FONTAINE to G.15.b. a few yards S.E. of the Red Tree, thence to about G.7.c.3.5.

27/10/18. 1 Company employed on clearing of Block at R.1.d.0.4.
2   "   employed on Defensive Support Positions.

28/10/18. The Defensive Support Position was amended and taped out by the Commanding Officer. New line taped out was from Road at G.8.a.3.7 via G.8.a.5.4 & G.8.a.4.0. across road to G.8.c.3.9.
2 Coys employed on the above Defensive Support Position.
1 Coy on clearing of Block at R.1.d.0.4.

29/10/18. Work was carried out as above detail.

30/10/18. 1 Coy clearing road at R.1.d.0.4. forward
1 Coy repairing road L.16.central – L.29.a. and L.24.a.0.0.
Cleaning of roads from Q.4.d.6.0. to Q.4.b.5.0. and the road from K.35.d.6.0. to L.29.a.
1 Coy completing work in hand on the Defensive Support Positions.

After work, one Company changed billets and moved to HONNECHY preparatory to being employed in Operations to be undertaken at a later date.

Sheet 2.

31/10/18.
1 Coy working on Bridge at R.1.d.0.4. which was opened for all traffic.
1 Coy working on Forward Roads.
1 Coy located at HONNECHY (Training).

Dispositions of the Battalion on the 31/10/18.

B.H.Q., Transport and 1 Company at ST.BENIN.
1 Company at R.1.d.0.4.
1 Company at HONNECHY.

All Map References are taken from Sheet 57 B.

1/11/18.
The Battalion was rested this day pending forthcoming operations, and all men were occupied in Special Training with the exception of "A" Coy who were located near MAZAL and responsible for the keeping open of the road from POMMEREUIL to FONTAINE for all traffic.

2/11/18.
Dispositions as on the 31/10/18. Special training for all Battalion except one Coy responsible for the maintenance of main POMMEREUIL - FONTAINE Road for all traffic and a special party detailed for the 105th Field Coy R.E. to unload lorries from dump for the Bridging Park.
There was a practice and demonstration at ST BENIN for the crossing of the SAMBRE-OISE CANAL a portion of the work being allotted to "B" Coy who were working in conjunction with 105th Field Coy R.E., 25th Division.

3/11/18.
November 3rd 1918 was known as 'Y' Day and in accordance with Operation Orders received movements as under were completed.
"B" Coy together with the 105th Field Coy R.E. moved from HONNECHY to their forward positions at L.26.a. and at dusk moved to assembly positions in Front Line, after which all materials were drawn from the advance dumps already prepared by "A" Coy.
"B" Coy with the R.Es were ready at midnight with the Infantry to commence the advance at ZERO hour which was at 5.45 am. on the 4th.
"C" Coy moved from ST.BENIN to the Railway Cutting in front of LE GATEAU.

4/11/18.
The 25th Division attacked on the 4/11/18 and Zero hour for the attack was at 5.45 am. The 25th Division were required to cross SAMBRE A L'OISE and capture LANDRECIES and to capture further objectives which involve the crossing of PETITE HELPE RIVER.
The following is the detail of work for this Battalion in connection with the above operations.
"B" Coy with the 105th Field Coy R.E. to ferry over the SAMBRE-OISE Canal. This operation was successfully completed and the Company then moved back to neighbourhood of POMMEREUIL.

"A" Coy at Zero plus 1 hour moved to L.28.a. and were held in reserve. This Coy supplied 3 N.C.Os & 24 men to work with "B" Coy bridging the SAMBRE-OISE CANAL.

"C" Coy were detailed to work on forward roads as under.
Coy moved on 'Y' day from ST.BENIN to Railway Cutting in vicinity of R.1.c.
They marched on 'Z' morning in time to start work from our present front line on that date at G.14.b. at Zero plus 2 hours.
Roads worked on - The POMMEREUIL - L.29.a. - MALGARNI - L.19.a.7.8. - G.13.d.7.0. - G.14.c.4.4. - G.20.a.8.5. - G.15.d.5.4. route.
MALGARNI-le-FAUX - G.13.b. 9.8. - G.20.a.8.5.
Le FAUX - FONTAINE-AUX-BOIS - FAUBOURG - BOYERS - LANDRECIES and subsequent to the crossing of the canal, forward roads as follows:-
MALGARNI - le- FAUX - LANDRECIES Rd, with special attention to road Junction and railway crossing in G.15.d.
Along the roads - Main Road LANDRECIES to MAROILLES and the road LANDRECIES - LA BLANCHISSERIE to OLD MILL BERES.

page 3.

3/11/18.	Advanced B.H.Q. opened at POMMEREUIL at 18.00 hours and on Z. day Advanced Report Centre moved at 05.00 hours at MALGARNI with 75th B.H.Q.
4/11/18.	A call was made on the Coy in reserve to supply 1 Platoon to maintain and keep open the Road POMMEREUIL to FONTAINE, particularly at FORRESTERS HOUSE & MALGARNI which was being heavily shelled. The Officer and 2 O.Rs reconnoitring the work were all wounded. Work commenced at 8.30 am. on Z day Also 1 Platoon warned to be held in readiness for work with the 130th Field Coy R.E. for the purpose of assisting in bridging of the PETITE HELPE RIVER.

Report received that O.C. "C" Coy (Capt M.D. Robinson) was wounded and heavy shelling experienced during assembly.
Work on Forward roads progressed well and Road party supplied men to assist R.E. Coy on approaches for two Pontoon bridges across Canal at LANDRECIES LOCK.

Orders received to move the whole of the Battalion (less "B" Coy) to FONTAINE au BOIS. Rear H.Q. Q.M. Stores, Transport & Coy Details accordingly moved forward at 8 pm from ST. REMIR.
"B" Coy remained for the night in Bivouacs near POMMEREUIL
1 Platoon of "A" Coy ordered at 10.15 pm to proceed to report to O.C. 130th Field Coy R.E. at L.18.a.8.6. for work until further orders.

5/11/18.	"B" Coy moved forward to FONTAINE au BOIS. Work carried as under on this date. 1 Coy. Filling in crater & making Corduroy track west of LANDRECIES on LANDRECIES-MAROILLES Main Road. 2 Coys. Clearing, draining & repairing main LANDRECIES-MAROILLES Rd
6/11/18.	1 Coy employed making approaches to Pontoon Bridges Les Mill Despres This Company moved to MAROILLES after work. 1 Platoon with 130 Field Coy R.E. bridging. 1 Coy moved to LANDRECIES and worked there on craters & roads. In the afternoon Coy moved to MAROILLES. 1 Coy worked on roads in front of LANDRECIES and billeted in the town. B.H.Q. moved in the morning from FONTAINE au BOIS to LANDRECIES and in the afternoon received orders to move immediately to MAROILLES with 2 Coys. This was done.
7/11/18.	1 Platoon Bridging with 130th Field Coy R.E. 3 Platoons on Bridge at DOMPIERE J.2.a.0.6. 1 Coy working on BARBAIX ROAD. Coy moved to TASNIERES. 1 Coy moved from LANDRECIES to MAROILLES in the morning and moved on to DOMPIERE in the afternoon.
8/11/18.	1 Coy worked on Craters on LANDRECIES-MAROILLES Rd. This Coy moved back to MAROILLES in order to be nearer the work and the 1 Platoon which had up to then been with the 130th Field Coy R.E. joined them there. 1 worked on Bridge and new road at TAISNIERES. 1 Coy worked on Corduroy track and crater in DOMPIERE Railway Station.
9/11/18.	Work carried out as on the 8/11/18.

Casualties incurred during the Operations under review as under:-

Officers wounded. Lieut. H.V. Worrall. 26/10/18.
 2nd Lieut. R. Carr. Missing 27/10/18.
 Captain M.D. Robinson. Wounded 4/11/18.
 2nd Lt. H. Jones. " " (Died of wounds).
 " " J. Kirkpatrick " "
 Lieut. L. Henshaw. Wounded, still duty 4/11/18.

O.Rs. Killed. 6. O.Rs Wounded. 32. Wounded still duty. 2.

Thompson Lt. Colonel

25
11 S Lanc R
Army Form C. 2118.

Vol 38

WAR DIARY
or
INTELLIGENCE SUMMARY.
(Erase heading not required.)

Place 1918	Date	Hour	Summary of Events and Information	Remarks and references to Appendices
	1.12.18		Batt" were shee at QUIEVY as per previous report.	
	11.12.18		His Majesty the King passed thro' QUIEVY at about 2.30 p.m. however The Battalion with the 4th Inf Bde formed up on the outer of the road & gave His Majesty 3 cheers. H.M. the King walked along the line & conversed with the officers & men.	
	16.12.18		The Batt" moved from QUIEVY to VIESLY & occupied Buses Billets	
	19.12.18		Latter place on same date. Information recd that the u/m men awarded immediate awards for operations during Nov 1918. Lt. S.E. Boulton M.C. Bar to M.C. Lieut L. Henwolaw M.C. 61090 Pte Redshaw Y. D.C.M. 20486 Pte S Humber M.M.	7.33
	19.12.18		115 ORs proceeded to internment centre Cambrai on date stated in margin to transfer to Army Reserve (Mining). On dates other than Wednesday & Saturday 4 Horses 2 Battalion employed on Training & Salvaging of Areas in vicinity of Billets	
	31.12.18		Strength 34 Offers 582 ORs.	

C. Champion
Maj 11 Bn S Lanc R C/O

Army Form C. 2118.

WAR DIARY
or
INTELLIGENCE SUMMARY.
(Erase heading not required.)

Place	Date	Hour	Summary of Events and Information	Remarks and references to Appendices
	1919			
	1 Jan		Battalion located at VIESLEY employed in Salvage & training until 12.1.19 when a move from VIESLEY was made to	
	13.1.19		SC: ESMES on 13.1.19. Battalion employed on Salvage work up to end of month. Demobilisation of the men of "B Cat" commenced 18/1/19 & 15 AF men were sent for dispersal up to end of month leaving "B Cat" strength on that date 437 OR. & 33 offers -	

C. Thompson L' Col
Cdg 11th Bn - Spaces Regt (Two)

Army Form C. 2118.

WAR DIARY
or
INTELLIGENCE SUMMARY.
(Erase heading not required.)

11th (S) BATTALION
SOUTH LANCS.
RGT. (PIONEERS)

Place	Date	Hour	Summary of Events and Information	Remarks and references to Appendices
	1919 Feb 1		The Battalion still at SOLESMES employed on Salvage work.	
	Feb 18		The Battalion moved from SOLESMES to ESCAUDOEUVRES on this date & occupied billets at the latter place, and employed on Salvage work.	
	26		Information received that the undermentioned had been awarded the "MILITARY MEDAL" No 4-8993 Sergeant H. McCOY	
	28		Demobilization of the Battalion has progressed steadily throughout the month. Number demobilized during Feby :- 7 Officers & 162 Other Ranks. Strength of the Battalion at end of month :- 26 Officers & 255 Other Ranks.	

Champion
Lt. Colonel
Commanding :- 11th Bn. SOUTH LANCS. REGT. (PIONEERS)

WAR DIARY
or
INTELLIGENCE SUMMARY.

Army Form C. 2118.

Vol 41

Place	Date	Hour	Summary of Events and Information	Remarks and references to Appendices
	1919 March 31		The Battalion still at ESCAUDEUVRES employed on Salvage Work.	
	Mar 22		Information received that the undermentioned had been awarded the "MEDAILLE BARRAINE St CAEDRIN" 3rd CLASS (Roumanian Decoration) No 20015 Private James March.	
	"	31	38 Other Ranks Re-enlisted under A.O. 14 of 10/3/18. 35 of which have been finally approved and sent to the U.K on furlough. 170 Other Ranks available for the Armies of Occupation under A.O 53 of 1919 and awaiting disposal, which leaves the Battalion at CAORE Strength.	
			Strength of the Battalion at end of month :- 19 Officers & 213 Other Ranks.	

C. Champion Lt Colonel
Commdg. 11th Bn. SOUTH LANCS. REGT. (PIONEERS)

Army Form C. 2118.

11TH (S) BATTALION
SOUTH LANCS.
REGT. (PIONEERS)

WAR DIARY
or
INTELLIGENCE SUMMARY.
(Erase heading not required.)

Instructions regarding War Diaries and Intelligence Summaries are contained in F. S. Regs., Part II. and the Staff Manual respectively. Title pages will be prepared in manuscript.

Place	Date	Hour	Summary of Events and Information	Remarks and references to Appendices
Cassel	1919 June	6	The Battalion Cadre located at Escauterre. Instructions received for the formation of a Battalion Cadre + an Equipment Guard.	
		8	The Bn. Cadre entrained at Bavinchove for dispatch to the U.K.	
			Entrained on 12th June 1919.	
		13	The Bn. Equipment Guard entrained at Bavinchove with baggage, Equipment and Stores on the 13th June 1919. The Guard on the completion of Equipment and the Cadre personnel duties will sent for dispatching home.	

E. Thompson Lieut Adjut
11th Bn. SOUTH LANCS REGT. (PIONEERS)

WAR DIARY
or
INTELLIGENCE SUMMARY.
(Erase heading not required.)

Army Form C. 2118.

11TH (S) BATTALION, SOUTH LANCS. REGT. (PIONEERS).

Place	Date	Hour	Summary of Events and Information	Remarks and references to Appendices
1919	April 1 to 30		The Battalion still located at ESCAUDŒUVRES and employed on Salvage work.	
	Apr 30		Total Re-enlistments to date is 41 all of which have been finally approved and sent to the U.K. on Re-enlistment furlough.	
			The Strength of the Battalion at the end of the month is as follows :—	
			Cadre 4 Officers and 41 Other Ranks.	
			Personnel eligible for Army of Occupation 7 Officers 144 Other Ranks	
			Volunteers for Army of Occupation 2 — —	
			Detached from Unit — — 165 Other Ranks	
			13 Officers and 165 Other Ranks	

C. Thompson Lieut. Colonel
Commdg. 11th Bn. SOUTH LANCS. REGT. (PIONEERS)

WAR DIARY or INTELLIGENCE SUMMARY

Army Form C. 2118.

Place	Date	Hour	Summary of Events and Information	Remarks and references to Appendices
	1919 MAY/31		The Battalion still located at ESCAUDŒUVRES.	43
	May 17		2 Officers left the Battalion to report for duty with the 69 P.O.W. Coy. ETAPLES.	
"	17		2 Officers left the Battalion to report for duty with the 191 P.O.W. Coy. ETAPLES.	
"	27		1 Officer & 70 O.Rs left the Battalion to report for duty with the 69 P.O.W. Coy. ETAPLES.	
"	28		1 Officer & 59 O.Rs left the Battalion to report for duty with the 191 P.O.W. Coy. ETAPLES.	
"			The remainder of O.Rs eligible for Army of Occupation are employed with the H.Q. Cambrai Sub-Area.	
"	29		5 O.Rs on reduction of Cadre establishment sent for dispersal.	
"	31		The strength of the Battalion at the end of month to as follows :- 6 Offs & 38 other Ranks.	

C. Thompson Lieut Colonel

Comdg.

11th Bn. SOUTH LANCS. REGT (PIONEERS)

30th Division

1st Lanc
Vol I
(Pioneer)

P/30

121/7795

V.1

Nov 15
|
Mar 18

Volume 1 November 1915

Confidential
War Diary
of
11th (S) Bn. S. Lancashire Regt
(St Helens Pioneers)

H Starrington Lt Colonel
Comdg 11th (S) Bn. S. Lancs Regt.
(Pioneers)

WAR DIARY
or
INTELLIGENCE SUMMARY

(Erase heading not required.)

Army Form C. 2118

Place	Date	Hour	Summary of Events and Information	Remarks and references to Appendices
Larkhill Camp.	6.11.15		Left Larkhill Camp on 6th Nov. for Southampton.	
S'hampton	6/11/15	5.0pm	Embarked on "MONAS QUEEN" & sailed at 5pm. Transport on "Invecta"	
HAVRE	6/11/15	12.0 M Night	Arrived at Havre at 12. midnight & disembarked at 8.0am on the 7.11.15.	
"	7/11/15	8.0am		
"	7/11/15	–	Proceeded to Rest Camp about 2 miles outside HAVRE.	
"	7/11/15	7.30pm	Left Rest Camp, Havre, at 7.30pm. and proceeded to place of Entrainment "GARE des MERCHANDISES"	
"	7/11/15	11.59pm	Left at 11.59 P.M. and arrived at PONTREMY at 6.30am on the 8.11.15. Strength:– arrived at PONTREMY 29 Officers 1007 O.Ranks	
Pont Remy	8/11/15	6.30am	1 Officer & 10 O.Ranks left behind at HAVRE as Divisional "Embark" officers	
"	8/11/15	7.30	Marched out of PONTREMY for Buscus Buscuel at 7.30am 8/11/15. In Full Marching Order plus Blanket & P. Sheet. about 8 miles from Station. (N0.5)	
Buscus Buscuel	8/11/15	4.0pm	Arr Buscus Buscuel about 4pm 8/11/15. Rest on way & a meal given 10 men. Road bad	
	16/11/15		Left Buscus Buscuel on the 16th Nov. for BETHENCOURT arriving & Billeted by 3pm. Departed on 17th Nov 7am YESSELLES at 1pm sauveclay	

WAR DIARY
or
INTELLIGENCE SUMMARY

(Erase heading not required.)

Army Form C. 2118

Place	Date	Hour	Summary of Events and Information	Remarks and references to Appendices
	17/11/15		On way from Berkencourt to Flesselles we met the 5th S. Lancs & formed up in line as 5th S. Lancs approached us we gave 3 Rousing Cheers for them, to which they heartily reciprocated, fellow'd by ½ hr for chat.	
FLESSELLES BERNEUIL	28/11/15 28/11/15	12.30	Left Flesselles 28th Nov 1915 at 9.10 am, arrived at BERNEUIL at 12.30 same day	

H Harvey Lt Colonel
Comg 11th S. Lancs Regt
(Pioneers)

v.2

The J. Law Co
Vol: 2

12/7809

30th K...

Acc 15.

Volume 2. December 1915

Secret

11th (S) Bn S Lancs Regt (Pioneers)

War Diary

for

December 1915.

31st Dec 1915   H Harrington   Lt Colonel
                Comdg 11th (S) Bn S Lancs Regt
                                (Pioneers)

WAR DIARY
or
INTELLIGENCE SUMMARY

(Erase heading not required.)

Army Form C. 2118

Place	Date	Hour	Summary of Events and Information	Remarks and references to Appendices
FLESSELLES	24/11/15		2 Coys (A&B) left for MAILLY MAILLET on 26/11/15 at 9.0 am for instruction in Trenches and attached to 10th Bde 4th Divn	
			Strgth 11 Officers 444 O.Ranks.	
MAILLY MAILLET			Returned from Trenches on 11th Decr. No casualties	
	28/11/15		C & D Coys Hd Qrs left Flesselles on 28/11/15 for BERNEUIL	
	6/12/15		"L" Coy left BERNEUIL for HALLOY-LES-PERNOIS for work on Horselandings in Artillery Area 6 Offrs & 223 O.R.	
	10/12/15		"C"-"D" Hd Qrs left on 10th Decr for training in Trenches attch'd 10th Bde - 4th Divn "C" Coy joined D Hd Qrs at Le Val de Maison at 12.45 on 10th Decr.	
	12/12/15		D Coy (7 Off + 134 OR) went in Trenches for 3 days & 3 nights C " (6 " & 165 ") working parties	
	13/12/15		C " 6 " ditto — 9 were sniped freely by enemy	
	14/12/15		C " 6 " ditto 2 men wounded through enemy sniping	
	15/12/15		C Coy go in trenches for 3 days & 3 nights Position of Coy	

WAR DIARY
or
INTELLIGENCE SUMMARY
(Erase heading not required.)

Army Form C. 2118

Place	Date	Hour	Summary of Events and Information	Remarks and references to Appendices
	18/12/15		D Coy working parties for Trenches. 2 men wounded by enemy snipers. 1 man killed by enemy sniper.	
	20/12/15		D Coy. 1 man killed by enemy sniper. 1 wounded – died 21/12/15 –	
	21/12/15		1 man died of Alcoholic Poisoning at BERNEUIL when on Guard. (Pte Pritchley) Hope Yr Guard remanded for F.G.C.M.	
	13 22/12/15		Enemy Aircraft over MAILLY MAILLET and dropped 2 Bombs in Village. 1 failed to go off, other exploded near Coy Billets but did no damage.	
	25/12/15	9.0 am	Left Mailly MAILLET on 25th Dec's for BERNEUIL via PUCHEVILLERS.	
	27/12/15	9.30 am	Left BERNEUIL as follows HQ Co & B Coy to PERNOIS "A" Coy Artillery Area "D" Coy HEM & HAR DINVAL "C" Coy to OUTREBOIS. Split up in this manner for various work on improvement to Billets &c.	
	31/12/15	11.30	L/C Smith to be tried by F.G.C.M. in BERNAVILLE starring for	

Cong!! 11th S. Lanc Regt
T. Colonel

1875. Wt. W 593/826 1,000,000 4/15 J.B.C. & A. A.D.S.S./Forms/C. 2118.

"Mrs Dawes.
Vol 3

Army Form C. 2118

WAR DIARY
or
INTELLIGENCE SUMMARY
(Erase heading not required.)

Instructions regarding War Diaries and Intelligence Summaries are contained in F. S. Regs., Part II. and the Staff Manual respectively. Title Pages will be prepared in manuscript.

Place	Date	Hour	Summary of Events and Information	Remarks and references to Appendices
	1/1/16		Battalion divided as per end of last summary	
Pernois	5/1/16		Left Pernois at 9.45 AM marched to NAOURS (A&B Coys+HqQs) C+D Coys meeting us there.	
	6/1/16		Bat'n left NAOURS at 8.50AM marched to PONT NOYELLES	
	7/1/16		Bat'n left PONT NOYELLES at 8.30am (less A Coy) & marched to CHIPILLY (C+D) & ETINEHAM (B+HQ's)	
			"A" Coy left PONT NOYELLES for PUCHEVILLERS for Railway work under T.R.C.E. 112th Railway Coy R.E.	
	8/1/16		Bat'n less "A" Coy marched to BRAY "D" (Coy proceeding to SUZANNE) B.C. & HQrs to FROISSY	
	11/1/16		"D" Coy at SUZANNE had 2 casualties (wounded in action) Enemy shelling Amiens there.	
	14/1/16		B.C. Coys working on BRAY-CORBIE Road, BONFAY Fme Light Railway Machine Gun Section proceeded to SUZANNE for work under G.O.C. 95th Brigade.	
FROISSY	21/1/16	6.50 am	Shelled by Enemy on 21/1/16 at irregular intervals 1 man wounded	
"	24/1/16	6 pm	5 Shells sent over 2 Mules wounded.	
"	25/1/16	3.20 pm	11 Shells sent over, no casualties.	

WAR DIARY
or
INTELLIGENCE SUMMARY

Army Form C. 2118

Place	Date	Hour	Summary of Events and Information	Remarks and references to Appendices
	26/1/16	3.50 p.m.	8 Shells over FROISSY	
		4.20 p.m.	5 " " "	
FROISSY	27/1/16	10.58 to 11 am	9 Shells No casualties. End of shut just behind Bn HQrs Blown in	
		2.23 pm	4 " (did not go off). Mark on fuze Cap HZ 14 T15. apparently fired by 10.5 Light Field Howitzer from direction of FAY.	
FROISSY	28/1/16	7.18 am to 4 p.m.	Continually shelled by Enemy, but the shells were somewhat over-ranged falling in a field behind the Bn Hq Qrs. 685 shells were sent over at an average of 1 per minute. 1 Man killed & 1 wounded. Ordered by Division (30th) to move out of FROISSY this being done about 4.30 p.m. At about 2 p.m. Artillery was exceedingly active, the enemy attempting to break through the left of the French lines & right of our lines.	
SUZANNE	28/1/16		1 man wounded of "D" Coy. This Coy under orders of G.O.C. 90th Bde	

WAR DIARY
or
INTELLIGENCE SUMMARY

(Erase heading not required.)

Instructions regarding War Diaries and Intelligence Summaries are contained in F.S. Regs., Part II. and the Staff Manual respectively. Title Pages will be prepared in manuscript.

Place	Date	Hour	Summary of Events and Information	Remarks and references to Appendices
BRAY	30/1/16		Working Parties detailed for urgent work at CAPPY placing houses in state of Defence, making Machine Gun Emplacements & Redoubts.	
	31/1/16		Ditto	
			Ditto	

Kavanagh
Lt Colonel
Comg 11th Shaves Regt
(Pioneers)

20 11th S. Lanes
Vol: 4

Confidential

War Diary

of

11th (S) Bn. Lancs Regt (Pioneers)

1st Feby 1916 to 29th Feby 1916

== Volume 4 ==

29/2/16

A Harington
Lt Colonel
Comg 11th Lancs Regt
(Pioneers)

Army Form C. 2118

WAR DIARY
or
INTELLIGENCE SUMMARY

(Erase heading not required.)

Instructions regarding War Diaries and Intelligence Summaries are contained in F.S. Regs., Part II. and the Staff Manual respectively. Title Pages will be prepared in manuscript.

Place	Date	Hour	Summary of Events and Information	Remarks and references to Appendices
BRAY.	3/2/16		On 3/2/16 "A" Coy arrived at ETINEHEM from PUCHEVILLERS and joined Battalion for duty. Left Billets in BRAY (BCoy & THQ) & moved to DUGOUTS. Position L8 Map 62C N.W. ALBERT.	
	7/2/16		"A" Coy took over duties from "D" Coy at SUZANNE.	
	9/2/16		"D" Coy moved to ETINEHEM	
	8/2/16		"D" Coy moved into DUGOUTS with Battalion HQ'rs	
	21/2/16		1 man wounded "A" Coy	
	29/2/16		1 " " " A " & 1 of "C" Coy	
			B " " died shortly after, 1 man wounded 'A' Coy	
			During month work on Communication Trenches & making Dugouts at SUZANNE & making Dugouts at Bn HQrs to take whole of Battalion. Continuation of work at CAPPY placing same in state of Defence, & work in Front Line Trenches.	

John L. Harrington Lt Colonel
Comg 11th Sherwood Foresters (Pioneers)

War Diary

11th (S) Bn S. Lancs Regt (Pioneers)

for

Month of March 1916

VOLUME No:
5

WAR DIARY
or
INTELLIGENCE SUMMARY

Army Form C. 2118

Place	Date	Hour	Summary of Events and Information	Remarks and references to Appendices
SUZANNE	1/3/16		1 Man 'A' Coy wounded at SUZANNE.	
BRAY	10/3/16		1 Man "B" " "	
SUZANNE	11/3/16		1 Man "A" " " 1 slightly but returned 12/3/16	
	15/3/16		'A' Coy rejoined Battn at Dugouts Grovetown Camp. Bray on 15/12 inst.	
	16/3/16		A & D Coys leave Dugouts & march to 7th Divn Area at MEAULTE	
			HQ Q's to VILLE sur ANCRE.	
			B & C Coy move out of Dugouts to Tents on Bank opposite to allow	
			the Sussex Regt Pioneers to occupy.	
MEAULTE	19/3/16		1 NCO & 2 men A Coy wounded by Shell fire. NCO suffered from Shell	
			Shock he has however returned to duty.	
			Major R H Gwyn Williams 2nd in Comd invalided to England 14/3/16	
	14/3/16		9 Struck off strength.	
			2 men wounded 'A' Coy owing to Keesdire since returned to duty	
MEAULTE	27/3/16		A & D Coys H.Q. move back to Tents at GROVETOWN CAMP.	
	31/3/16		Comg Officer Sick & has to leave Batn for rest Major T Potter taking	
			over Command from that date	

T. Potter, Major O.C.
11th S Lancs Regt (Pioneers)

War Diary
of
11th S.Lancs Regt. (Pioneers)

Vol. No 6

April 1916

Army Form C. 2118

WAR DIARY
or
INTELLIGENCE SUMMARY

(Erase heading not required.)

Vol 6

Place	Date	Hour	Summary of Events and Information	Remarks and references to Appendices
	3/3/16		A&D Coys & Hd Qrs left Meaulte & Ville respectively & went back to GROVETOWN. (under Canvas).	
	3/4/16		Dug new fire trench in front of front line at Pt J 11 & J 11³ from 6.30pm to 5am. 298 NCOs & men of B&C Coys. 7 Officers took part. Trench completed manned by 21st Manchester Regt.	
	18/4/16		Working Parties carried on Day & night	
	27/4/16		Move back to VAUX en AMIENOIS for rest. Inspection by Divisional Comr Major Genl Watts C.V.C.B. On Parade. 25 Officers 856 Other Ranks. at 9.30 a.m.	

Kenny ?on
Lt Col
Comg 11th Lancs Regt (Govel Reserve)

Confidential

War Diary
— of the —
11th (S) Bn. South Lancs Regt. (Pioneers)

1st May 1916 — to — 31st May 1916

(Volume 7).

Army Form C. 2118

WAR DIARY
or
INTELLIGENCE SUMMARY
(Erase heading not required.)

Vol 7.

Place	Date	Hour	Summary of Events and Information	Remarks and references to Appendices
VAUX en-AMIENOIS	2/5/16	8.30 a.m.	B & C Coys under Capt Forester left for Bois de Celestine & Chipilly. C Coy + ½ B Coy on road work under officer i/c Roads 13th Corps at Bois de Taillés; ½ B Coy under O.C. 1st & 2nd Coy	
	3/5/16	4.0 p.m.	A & D Coys & H.Q. & Staff Vaux en Amienois at 4 pm for Corbie & billeted there for the night.	
CORBIE.	4/5/16	4.0 p.m.	Left Corbie at 4.0 pm for Grovetown Camp.	
	6/5/16	4.30 p.m.	B & C Coys rejoined Batt'n at Grovetown Camp. C Coy went on to SUZANNE.	
	7/5/16		B Coy to "Z" Ravine.	
	6/5/16		A Coy (2 platoons) went to SUZANNE.	
	12/5/16		77 NCO's & men 'C' Coy engaged on Rescuework in Trench Y3 commencing 5.30pm on 11th & continuing in hourly reliefs until 13/5/16.	
	13/5/16		1 man 'A' Coy wounded (Shrapnel). returned to duty 29/5/16.	
	19/5/16		1 " C " " " " "	
	19/5/16		1 " D " " " " "	
	23/5/16		1 " B " " slightly. returned to duty 27/5/16.	

WAR DIARY
or
INTELLIGENCE SUMMARY

Army Form C. 2118

(Erase heading not required.)

Place	Date	Hour	Summary of Events and Information	Remarks and references to Appendices
	19/5/16		1 Platoon "B"Coy moved to "J" Ravine on 19th inst.	
	30/5/16		2 Platoons "A" Coy & remainder "B" Coy moved to TRIGGER VALLEY	
	31/5/16		Distribution of Batn evening of 31/5/16:- 11 Platoons in Trigger Valley 5 " in "J" Ravine. Bn Hd Qrs in GROVETOWN DUGOUTS.	
	16/5/16		Lt.Col. Sir J.H. Harrington K.C.M.G, K.C.V.O, C.B., comdg Batn went to England (Sick Leave) whilst there received notification from XIIICorps that he had received appointment as Commandant at ARDRICQUE	
	26/5/16		Lt.Col. H.F. Fenn (late 21st Royal Fus rs) reported & took over command of Battalion.	

H.F. Fenn Lt. Colonel
Comdg XI. S Lancs Regt
(Pioneers)

CONFIDENTIAL.

WAR DIARY

OF

11th (S) Bn. SOUTH LANCASHIRE REGIMENT. (PIONEERS)

FROM

1st JUNE 1916 to 30th JUNE 1916.

(VOLUME No 8).

WAR DIARY or INTELLIGENCE SUMMARY

Army Form C. 2118

Place	Date	Hour	Summary of Events and Information	Remarks and references to Appendices
	1/6/16		Dist of Batt. TRIGGER VALLEY 11 Platoons (A.Y. Coy & 3 pns D Coy)	
			⅟ RAVINE 4 " (B Coy)	
			In Dugouts 1 " (D Coy) N E of Bray.	
			Bn HQ TRIGGER VALLEY.	
	31/5/16		QM Stores & Transport BRAY.	
	3/6/16		2 men wounded 1 of C 1 of D.	
	6/6/16		1 NCO (B Coy) wounded.	
	4/6/16		Capt. L. E. Champion appd Temp Major & 2nd in Command of Battn effect from 14/4/16	
			21435 Sgt P. McGowan 'B' Coy tried by F.G. Court Martial for "When on Active Service	
			Drunkenness" Sentence "Reduced to the Ranks.	
			Lt & QM Rice Struck off strength effect from 2/6/16	
			2Lt Y Craig transferred to 3 Hussars 6/6/16.	
	8/6/16		2 men wounded (B) Coy	
	15/6/16		Lt G H Walker transferred to R.F.C. 15/6/16.	
	"		4 men wounded (B Coy)	
	11/6/16		2/Lt A.G.R. Hawkes invalided to England.	

Army Form C. 2118

WAR DIARY
or
INTELLIGENCE SUMMARY
(Erase heading not required.)

Instructions regarding War Diaries and Intelligence Summaries are contained in F. S. Regs., Part II. and the Staff Manual respectively. Title Pages will be prepared in manuscript.

Place	Date	Hour	Summary of Events and Information	Remarks and references to Appendices
	3/6/16.		20086 Pte Pouncely W "B" Coy awarded Military Medal vide London Gazette. (to be taken to Battn since coming overseas).	
			Lt Col Sir J. Hannington KCMG. KCVO. CB. late CO of Battn & 20313 RSM Boden J. mentioned in dispatch by Genl Sir Douglas Haig. GCB. C. in Chief British forces in France. dated 30/4/16.	
	21.6/16		21469 Pte Roberts H. "B" Coy thro' Negligence caused Self Inflicted Wound & tried by H.q. C. M.	
	22/6		1 man B Coy Killed	
	23/6		Battn left for Bray l'ETINEHEM. C in C op to former place A/B MHQ to latter. A/B MHQ move to BRAY.	
	26/6		1 man A Coy Killed	
	23/6		1 " C " " 1 NCO wounded 1 man B Coy Drown.	
	26/6			
	30/6/16		Work during month June 1916. chiefly in Trenches preparing for British Advance originally fixed for June 25th 1916 but postponed to 10th July. Battn assembled in trenches at various fixed points by 7-30 pm 30/6/16 1 man B Coy self inflicted wound – shot himself thro' finger about 1 hour prior to Coy moving up to trenches. To be tried by H.q. C.M.	

A. Kerr
Lt Colonel
11th S. Lancs Regt. (Pioneers)

11 Slanes
July 1916

CONFIDENTIAL.

WAR DIARY
of
11th Bn. SOUTH LANCASHIRE REGIMENT. (PIONEERS)

from 1st July 1916 to 31st July, 1916.

VOLUME 9.

Army Form C. 2118

WAR DIARY
or
INTELLIGENCE SUMMARY
(Erase heading not required.)

Instructions regarding War Diaries and Intelligence Summaries are contained in F.S. Regs., Part II. and the Staff Manual respectively. Title Pages will be prepared in manuscript.

Place	Date	Hour	Summary of Events and Information	Remarks and references to Appendices
	30.7.15.		Battn Headquarters changed to COPSE RAVINE evening of the 30th June, 1916. All parties in position by 7-25 p.m. viz.	
		1	"A" Coy 2 Platoons assembled in "U" Works N of Peronne Rd	
		2	" " 2 " " " "U" ditto.	
		3	"B" Coy 2 " " Trenches in MARICOURT(S) East Face of NAPIER KEEP (300x of trench)	
		4	" " 2 " " COPSE VALLEY as Divisional Reserve.	
		5	"C" Coy 4 " " Trenches in MARICOURT(S) (East Face of NAPIER KEEP(ditto)	
		6	"D" Coy 1 " " Trenches in MARICOURT(N) (East Face & part of South Face of	
			(CHATEAU KEEP(140x of Trench)	
		7	" " 1 " " DIXONS DITCH Trench.	
		8	" " 1 " " STANLEY & MARICOURT AVENUES. (Maintenance Parties)	
		9	" " 1 " " SUPPORT & WEST AVENUES. (ditto.)	
		1	Objective. To open Communication Trench From Sap No 6 (A/9/3) Support Aven)	
		2.	" To open " " From Sap No 5 (A/9/4) West Aven)	
		3.	" To open " " From Sap No 3 to German Wood (Stanley Aven)	
		4.	" Divisional Reserve.	
		5.	" To open Communication Trench from Sap A.P. 4 to enemy's trenches & onwards	
			(Maricourt Aven)	
		6.	" Prepare Strong Points at A 10 d 1/6 & A 10 a 4/6	
		7.	" " " " A 3 d 6/2.	
		8 & 9	Maintenance of Communication Trenches and opening of Russian Saps on evening of 1.7.16 Lewis Gun Section assembled in "U" works on the 30th June and did not move during operations	
	1.7.16		The Battalion took part in the Offensive carried out by the 30th Division on the right of the British front. Hour of Zero 7-30 a.m. 1st July, 1916) The duties and objectives allotted to the Battalion as above were carried out to time. At 2-45 p.m. on 1st July 2 Communication Trenches were through to German Front Line to a depth of 4 feet. (Nos 2 and 4 from right of sector) At 3-43 P.m. No 1 Communtn Trench was open to a depth of 5 ft. All these 5 were immediately continued and work progressed favourably. No 3 was not ready till much later owing to heavy casualties from Shell fire. At 9-20 p.m. Russian Saps were opened by Trench Communication Parties. Saps from A.P. 3 & 4 and A.P. 5 & 6.	

1875. Wt. W593/826 1,000,000 4/15 J.B.C. & A. A.D.S.S./Forms/C.2118.

WAR DIARY
or
INTELLIGENCE SUMMARY
(Erase heading not required.)

Army Form C. 2118

Instructions regarding War Diaries and Intelligence Summaries are contained in F.S. Regs., Part II. and the Staff Manual respectively. Title Pages will be prepared in manuscript.

-2-

Place	Date	Hour	Summary of Events and Information	Remarks and references to Appendices
			Parties also povided on MONTAUBAN - MARICOURT ROAD.	
	2.7.16.	2-5 p.m.	O.C. Sap Working party reported the Saps A.P. 5 and A.P. 6 were uncovered by 2-5 p.m At Sap A.P. 6 the sap fell in a great deal and so caused the trench to be rather wider than it ought to be. Owing to the bad state of trench East side of MARICOURT-BRIQUETERIE road in the old German lines the communication trench was fixed from A.P. 3 to run via strong point 1/89 along east side of GERMANS WOOD to CASEMENT TRENCH.	
		7-25 p.m.	Communication trench from No 5 sap A 9/4 1 now useable up to strong point 4/21.	
		7-30 p.m.	Communication trench from Sap No 6 A 9/3 useable to strong point 1/21. Communication Trench from A.P. 4 via strong points 2/89 through to strong point 2/21 in DUBLIN TRENCH.	
	5.7.16.		Officer i/c Strong Points 1/89 and 2/89 reported work still continues on Strong Points 1/89 and 2/89. Strong Point 1/89 was heavily shelled on night of 2nd and work was therefore impossible. On examination later it was found that through shelling much damage has been done especially to face work. Shelling still continued at 11-30 a.m. when work on top is attempted particularly. By 3 p.m. all was clear from Sap A.P. 4 and good useable trench through to DUBLIN TRENCH.	
			On the 1st July when our Parties followed the Infantry over the parapet many casualties were caused through the Division on the left being held up. Quite a number of them were caused through Machine Gun fire from the enemy.	
	4.7.16: 7.7.16:		On the 4th instant the Battalion went back to rest billets in the BOISE de TAILLES On the 7th July 2 Coys were ordered back to the line to be under orders of 21st Brigade. 1 Coy at disposal of 2nd Bn Yorks Regt and other Coy remained in 2nd Reserve in Assembly Trenches. Work under orders of 21st Brigade who were to capture Southern end of the TRONES WOOD and establish connection with a French attack Result Coy with 2nd Yorks did very little serious work. Prior to this move however, viz 5th July 1916 2 Coys were employed on the preparatory work of Cutting lanes from West to East through the Southern portion of ERNAFAY WOOD.	
	8.7.16.		Hd Qrs and 2 Coys moved up to COPSE VALLEY, the other 2 Coys joining on the 9 and 10th	

Army Form C. 2118

WAR DIARY
or
INTELLIGENCE SUMMARY
(Erase heading not required.)

Instructions regarding War Diaries and Intelligence Summaries are contained in F.S. Regs., Part II. and the Staff Manual respectively. Title Pages will be prepared in manuscript.

Place	Date	Hour	Summary of Events and Information	Remarks and references to Appendices
	8.7.16.		Two Coys placed at disposal of O.C. 21st Brigade to dig trenches and on road work.	
	9.7.16.		Disposition of Coys. 2 Coys working under direct orders of 21st Brigade and 2 Coys who went to Glatz Redoubt night of 8th and were not required, in COPSE VALLEY minus 1 platoon on Road work under 258th Coy R.E. Maricourt.	
	12.7.16.		Battalion, less 1 Coy left at disposal of G.O.C. 18th Division for work on the BRIQUETERIE ROAD) proceeded to GROVETOWN for rest. 1 draft received of 7 Officers from 14th (S) Bn Worcester Regt. 1 Coy under orders of G.O.C. 18th Division rejoined Battalion.	
	19.7.16		Battn moved to HAPPY VALLEY	
	20.7.16.		Battalion moved to TALUS BOISE area.	
	22.			

M. Jun
Lt. Colonel
Commanding 11th S. Lancs Regt. (Pioneers).

11th (S) Bn. South Lancashire Regt. (Pioneers).

BRIEF ACCOUNT OF WORK DONE BY THIS BATTALION
DURING OPERATIONS 20th to 30th JULY (Inclusive) 1916.

July 20th.	Resting at GROVETOWN and moved to HAPPY VALLEY.
July 21st.	Still in HAPPY VALLEY resting.
July 22nd.	Moved at night to TALUS BOISE Area in accordance with O.O. No 26, as Divisional Reserve, with an Officer representing the Battn at 21st Brigade and 89th Brigade Headquarters.
July 23rd.	No orders received from Brigades, therefore no work done.
July 24th.	One Platoon worked on Div. Headquarters Dug-outs. Remainder of Battn worked on CABLE TRENCH from BRIQUETERIE to TRONES WOOD. Average depth 3 feet.
July 25th.	One Platoon worked on Divl Headquarters Dugouts. CABLE TRENCH from Signal Station, BRIQUETERIE along North side of SUNKEN ROAD to BERNAFAY ALLEY dug. Cable Trench from TRONES WOOD to BRIQUETERIE dug to depth of 5 feet, except 300 yards dug only 3ft 6 inches.
July 26th.	One Platoon worked on Divisional Headquarters Dugouts. Trench from GLATZ REDOUBT to SIGNAL STATION, BRIQUETERIE and on to SUNKEN ROAD, dug. 300 yards of CABLE TRENCH from BRIQUETERIE to TRONES WOOD dug to an average depth of 5 ft. CABLE TRENCH along SUNKEN ROAD lengthened to A 5 d 76.96 dug.
July 27th.	One Platoon worked on Divl Headquarters Dugouts. "C" Coy cut one track through TRONES WOOD 120 yards South of Railway. CABLE TRENCH from TRONES WOOD to BRIQUETERIE completed to depth of 6 feet and floor levelled. CABLE TRENCH along SUNKEN ROAD to A 5 d 76.96 deepened and levelled.
July 28th.	One Platoon worked on Divl Headquarters Dugouts. Trench between BERNAFAY WOOD & TRONES WOOD running N to S about 450 yards long dug. Average depth 4 feet. One Assembly Trench 4 feet deep 120 yards long dug on right of GUILLEMONT ROAD 200 yards E of TRONES WOOD. Reliefs working on Dugouts by BRIQUETERIE in Sunken Road.
July 29th.	One Platoon worked on Divisional Headquarters Dugouts. Two Assembly Trenches dug in front of N.E. side of TRONES WOOD. Average depth 3 ft 9 in and a parapet of 2 ft. Both 120 yds long. One Assembly trench dug on the right of GUILLEMONT ROAD in front of TRONES WOOD. Average depth 4 ft 120 yards long. Four paths through TRONES WOOD finished and clearly defined with strips of Calico. Reliefs still working on Dugouts near BRIQUETERIE in Sunken Road.
July 30th.	Reliefs worked all day on Dugouts Near BRIQUETERIE in Sunken Road 2 Officers as representatives of this Battalion reported, one to 89th Brigade and one to 90th Brigade Headquarters. Battn awaited orders for work in connection with O.O. No 28 dated 28th July 1916

31st July 1916.   Lieut Colonel.
                                    Comdg 11th S. Lancs Regt. (Pioneers).

Trenches &c Dug by 11th S.Lancs Rgt. since offensive of 1.7.16.

SECRET. Copy No 44

Those marked over in Black
Dug by 11th S Lancs Regt. on 1st 3rd
July 1916.

30th Divisional Pioneers

1/11th BATTALION

SOUTH LANCASHIRE REGIMENT

AUGUST 1 9 1 6

WAR DIARY
or
INTELLIGENCE SUMMARY
(Erase heading not required.)

Place	Date	Hour	Summary of Events and Information	Remarks and references to Appendices
	1.8.16		Battn resting in HAPPY VALLEY after the previous months operations. Casualties during operations of July 1916 amounting to 190 Other Ranks.	
	2.8.16.		Battn away from Fighting Area to Rest in Back Area viz HALLENCOURT. Entrained at MERICOURT STN for LONGPRE. Arrived late at night and marched to HALLENCOURT arriving there about 2-30 a.m. on the 3.9.16. Received orders that we should move on the 4th instant.	
	3.8.16. 4.8.16.		Battn left HALLENCOURT for PONT REMY Station and thence by rail to MERVILLE. Battn arrived at MERVILLE Station had to march back to MOLINGHEM arriving about 11-30 p.m. Remained at MOLINGHEM until 10th instant when Battn moved at 4 a.m. in the morning en route	
	10.8.16		for GORRE, where we arrived about noon after a 15 miles march.	
			11th 12th 13th utilised by men for cleaning up generally.	
	14.8.16		Battn started work in new area viz FESTUBERT & GIVENCHY areas. "A" Coy right sector of line under under 202nd Field Coy. R.E. "B" " left sector of line do. 200th do. "C" " village line under O.C. 201st Field Coy R.E. "D" " on Drainage of the 30th Divisional area	
	15.8.16.		"A" Coy had 4 Casualties on the 1st day in the line (Wounded). "A" " had 2 more casualties wounded. "B" " had 1 Killed & 5 Wounded.	
	22.8.16. 23.8.16. 24.8.16		2 Men of "A" Coy wounded. 5 Officers joined Battn ex 1/3rd Mormouth Regt(T.F.) The General Officer Commanding, First Army, presented on the 24th instant, on parade, the riband of the Military Medal awarded to No 20089 Pte J.FRODSHAM of this Battn "A" Coy for gallantry and devotion to duty. Strength of Battn on the 31st August 1916 Other Ranks 887. (actually with Bn).	

Ccmdg 11th (S) Bn. S.Lancashire Regt.(Pioneers).

Lt.Colonel.

Confidential

War Diary

of

11ᵗʰ (S) Bⁿ South Lancashire Regt.

from

1ˢᵗ Septʳ 1916 to 30ᵗʰ Septʳ 1916

(Volume No 11).

Army Form C. 2118

WAR DIARY
or
INTELLIGENCE SUMMARY
(Erase heading not required.)

Instructions regarding War Diaries and Intelligence Summaries are contained in F.S. Regs., Part II. and the Staff Manual respectively. Title Pages will be prepared in manuscript.

Place	Date	Hour	Summary of Events and Information	Remarks and references to Appendices
	1.9.16.		Battalion still in the FESTUBERT & GIVENCHY Sectors as per Report of last month.	
	6.9.16.		Battalion billetted in GORRE.	
	9.9.16.		Received a Draft of 16 O.Ranks. Received very urgent orders to be prepared to Move to 17th Corps Area at 1 hours notice. However did not move off until 6 p.m. on the 10th, and marched to BETHUNE Station and there entrained for AUBIGNY Station, and afterwards marched to EQUIVRES arriving there in the early hours of the morning on the 10th.	
	11.9.16.		Coys orders to proceed to points as follows for work "A" Coy to FORT GEORGE. "C" & "D" Coys to NEUVILLE ST VAAST. "B" Coy to the EMPIRE & PYLONES.	
	15.9.16.		Received a draft of 1 Officer (Q.M.) and 4 O.Ranks. Received urgent orders to again move.	
	16.9.16.		Marched to ACQ about 1 mile and stayed there the day.	
	17.9.16.		Left ACQ and marched to GAMBLIGNEUIL.	
	19.9.16.		Left CAMBLIGNEUIL and marched to SAVY Station and entrained for DOULLENS and re-joined the 30th Division. Marched from DOULLENS to LONGUEVILLETTE.	
	21.9.16.		Left LONGUEVILLETTE and marched to HAVERNAS where the whole of the 30th Division were round about resting.	
	22.9.16. to 25.9.16.		Coys doing Coy Drill and general training.	
	27.9.16.		Battalion left 30th Division, and moved to 15th Corps area by Busses (DERNANCOURT).	
	28.9.16.		Battalion marched from DERNANCOURT to MONTAUBAN via Albert, Fricourt, Mametz and MONTAUBAN in Bell Tents, position about 3 26 B.8.3. near MONTAUBAN. The Germans evidently having noticed the Tents being erected by means of his Observation Balloon shelled during the night in the vicinity. Struck camp at 6 a.m. next morning and moved to various shelters in trenches. 1 man wounded of "A" Coy. Time during the month taken up chiefly with preparing to move and actually moving. Received a letter of congratulation from G.O.C. XVII Corps on the work done by the Battalion during the short stay with them.	
			Battalion about 69 Other Ranks under strength on the 30th and 14 Officers under strength.	

M Lee
Lt.Colonel.
Comdg 11th S. Lancs Regt.(Pioneers).

CONFIDENTIAL.

WAR DIARY

OF

11th (S) BATTN. SOUTH LANCASHIRE REGT. (PIONEERS)

from

OCTOBER 1st, 1916 to 31st OCTOBER, 1916

VOLUME 12.

Army Form C. 2118

WAR DIARY
or
INTELLIGENCE SUMMARY
(Erase heading not required.)

Instructions regarding War Diaries and Intelligence Summaries are contained in F.S. Regs., Part II. and the Staff Manual respectively. Title Pages will be prepared in manuscript.

Place	Date 1916	Hour	Summary of Events and Information	Remarks and references to Appendices
	1.10.		Battn at MONTAUBAN under orders of 41st Division, for work on roads, at BAZENTIN.	
	5.10.		2 Coys laying Duckboards in Fish Alley & Goose Alley, in forward area (Map ref M 30 a 6.4. & M 36 b 5.4.).	
	8.10.		2 Coys on road work, 3 platoons on night work in GOOSE ALLEY (clearing obstructions) and 1 Platoon on TURK LANE. 3 Platoons clearing obstructions in portions of FISH ALLEY. Working from ABBEY ROAD to the rear.	
	9.10.		Battalion ordered to move to a new area at BAZENTIN-le-GRAND, and on arriving there no suitable place to be found anywhere, other Battalions and Bde Hdqrs being there, consequently Battalion received orders to stay where it was prior to moving to Bazentin-le-Grand.	
	10.10.		Battalion under orders of 30th Division.	
	12.10.		Battalion moved up to Assembly trench in 21st Bde area S 5 a 6.4. at 2 p.m. also Advcd Bn Hdqrs 4-30 p.m. Coys left to assemble in trenches for work at 6 p.m. each party sending an Officer and some men ahead to reconnoitre the ground to be worked, in connection with the Offensive to be taken by the 30th Division.	
		6-50 p.m.	following position and distribution of Battn. Advcd Hdqrs at S 5 a 6.4. Lewis Gunners under 21st Brigade at S 5 b 7.3. 2 Coys in Fish Alley at N 25 c 6.9. 2 Coys in Goose Alley. Coy unable to wer go out to dig trenchs as per Operation Order No 40 owing to unfavourable situation. Orders then received from C.R.E. 30th Div for Coys to work on FISH ALLEY, PIONEER LANE & GOOSE ALLEY, behind our old front line. A & C Coys then carried out following work. 2 Coys dug 400 yds of extension of Fish Alley to advance average depth of 4ft 6inches N 25 c 2.2 to N 25 c 6.9. and deepened 400 yds to a depth of 5' 6" M 36 b 5.6 to N 25 c 2.2. 2 Platoons dug new trench 140 yards long and 6 ft deep from end of GOOSE ALLEY M 24 b 6.6 to a trench or strong point held by 17th Kings Liverpool Regt at M 24 b 7.8. Remaining 1½ Coys at S 5 a 6.4. with Advcd Headquarters.	
	13.10.	2-30 a.m.	orders sent out to Coys to return at once.	
	13.10.		Battalion ordered to go forward again for purposes of digging trench to front line. Disposition. Turk Lane from Goose Alley along Abbey Rd. Result 1232 yds dug 5 feet deep 2ft bottom 4 ft top from point M 30 a 5.7. Junct of Turk Lane & Goose Alley.	
	14.10.		"A" Coy and 2 Platoons of B on night work on FISH ALLEY extending it so as to be clear of Factory Corner avoiding all German trenches where possible. (idea, to avoid the possibilities of enemy artillery knowing the exact range of their old trenches and consequently shelling them thinking that Infantry etc would use them for assembly)	

Army Form C. 2118

WAR DIARY
or
INTELLIGENCE SUMMARY
(Erase heading not required.)

Instructions regarding War Diaries and Intelligence Summaries are contained in F. S. Regs., Part II. and the Staff Manual respectively. Title Pages will be prepared in manuscript.

Place	Date	Hour	Summary of Events and Information	Remarks and references to Appendices
	15.10.		2 Platoons "B" Coy on night work clearing out FISH ALLEY. "D" Coy on night work clearing out and completing GOOSE ALLEY.	
"	18.10.		Work done night 14th/15th Digging and extending FISH ALLEY 250 Yds (new dug) Clearing up trench -FERRET TCH - to ABBEY RD 400 yds average depth 5½ feet. Clearing and deepening GOOSE ALLEY for 450 yards. Division continue offensive. Battalion moved to forward area also advcd H.Qrs in CREST TRENCH Result of operation. 500 yards fire trench traversed and dug average depth 4'3" from end of TURK LANE to approx M 17 d central, & Fire trench traversed dug from M 24 a 8.2. about 500 yds.	
	20.10.		Battn Lewis Gunners ordered to report to 21st Bde Hdqrs and to be attached to one of their Battalions to assist in the Line.	
	21.10.		1 Coy on TURK LANE, cleared from Front Line to about 100 yards South of GOOSE ALLEY, Sump holes dug at about 20 yds interval and trench boards laid over sumps. 1 Coy on TURK LANE - from Eaucourt L'ABBAYE RD to SUNKEN ROAD in M 35 , cleared and sump holes dug. 1 Coy on FISH ALLEY 450-500 yds of trench cleaned and about 12 sump holes dug, starting from the FACTORY - EAUCOURT L'ABBAYE RD and going South. 1 Coy on FISH ALLEY 1000 yards 11n widened deepened and made passable for Stretchers average depth 5'6".	
	22.10.		Battalion left vicinity of MONTAUBAN (Map ref S 26 b 8.7.) for DERNANCOURT CAMP, N of Dernancourt.	
	23.10.		Battalion returned on the 24th to vicinity of MONTAUBAN (Map Ref S 26 b 5.5.) for work on railways under the R.C.E. 4	
	25.10.		Work continued on Railways until the 5th 11.16 when Battalion rejoined 30th Div on the 6.11.16.	

M. Penn Lt Colonel.

Comdg 11th S. Lancs Regt.(Pioneers).

CONFIDENTIAL.

WAR DIARY

OF

11th (S) Bn. SOUTH LANCASHIRE REGIMENT. (PIONEERS).

--- from ---

1st NOVEMBER, 1916

--to--

30th NOVEMBER, 1916.

VOLUME 13.

Army Form C. 2118

WAR DIARY
or
INTELLIGENCE SUMMARY
(Erase heading not required.)

Instructions regarding War Diaries and Intelligence Summaries are contained in F.S. Regs., Part II. and the Staff Manual respectively. Title Pages will be prepared in manuscript.

Place	Date	Hour	Summary of Events and Information	Remarks and references to Appendices
	1916			
	6.11.		Battalion arrived at HUMBERCOURT by Bus from TALMAS, and stayed in billets until the 9th,	
	9.11.		when Battalion marched out to forward area to take over work from Monmouths. Battalion distributed as follows:- Headquarters, 2 Ptns of "A" Coy B Coy & D Coy billetted at BERLES-au-Bois, 2 Platoons of "A" Coy, Qr.Mrs stores and Transport at LA CAUCHIE and "C" Coy at BAILLEULVAL. O.C. responsible for the Defence of BERLES-au-BOIS in case of attack by the enemy, on and from the 9th inst, when Monmouths left the area.	
	10.11.		Work carried on as taken over from Monmouths viz., Divisional Line and Defences of Village of BERLES-AU-BOIS with the exception of 2 Ptns of "A" Coy on Roads in LA CAUCHIE area and "C" Coy on roads in BAILLEULVAL area. Work carried on for the month, with the exception of inter-Coy reliefs on various works and roads. Only 3 Casualties occurred during the month of Novr.1916 all of which were wounded. "Gas" used by the British on our Divisional front on the night of the 12th inst, but no ill effects felt as far back as BERLES-au-BOIS.(about 1,800 yds from front line). The "GAS ALERT" has been in force on frequent occasions during the last few days, the wind being favourable for enemy discharge of "Gas".	
	5.12.16.			

C.C.Champion Major for Lt.Col.(A.O.I.)
Comdg 11th S. Lancs Regt.(Pioneers).

11th (S) Bn. South Lancashire Regt.(Pioneers).

WAR DIARY

OF

the

11th (S) BN. S. LANCS. REGT.(PIONEERS).

1st Decr.1916. to 31st Decr. 1916.

VOLUME No. 14.

From O.C.
    11th S Lancs Regt (Pioneers)

To D A G,
    3rd Echelon.

———"———

Herewith Vol 8 "War Diary" of the Battalion under my Command for month of June 1916.

              H. Fenn Lt Colonel

3/7/16   Comg 11th S Lancs Regt
                  (Pioneers)

Army Form C. 2118

WAR DIARY
or
INTELLIGENCE SUMMARY

(Erase heading not required.)

Place	Date	Hour	Summary of Events and Information	Remarks and references to Appendices
	1916 1.12.		Battalion distributed as follows:- Bn. Hd.qrs. B & D Coys & ½ "A" Coy at Berles-au-Bois. "C" Coy at Grosville & Transport at La Cauchie. With the exception of Inter-Coy relieves during the month, work carried on, on the Divisional Line & roads as last month. Work commenced on a new Strong Point "Panets Post" & finished with the exception of a few minor details.	
	13.12.		Owing to our Artillery Operations on the 13th Decr. 1916, men ordered to Bombardment Stations in Berles from 10 a.m. to 3 p.m. on that date, in case the enemy should retaliate on the village.	
	24.12.		Enemy artillery very active, trying apparently to find some Big Guns (Siege battery) in position behind Battn Headquarters and again on the 29th Decr. 1916, the enemy artillery shelled Berles heavily.	
	25.12.		The Battalion rested on Xmas day, no work being done.	

Lt.Colonel.

Comdg 11th S. Lancs Regt.(Pioneers).

11th (S) Bn. South Lancashire Regt.(Pioneers).

WAR DIARY
of
the
11th (S) Bn. South Lancashire Reg.
(Pioneers)

1st January,1917 to 31st January,1917.

Volume No.15.

Army Form C. 2118

WAR DIARY
or
INTELLIGENCE SUMMARY
(Erase heading not required.)

Instructions regarding War Diaries and Intelligence Summaries are contained in F. S. Regs., Part II. and the Staff Manual respectively. Title Pages will be prepared in manuscript.

Place	Date 1917	Hour	Summary of Events and Information	Remarks and references to Appendices
In the Field BERLES-au-BOIS	8/1/17		Batt moved from forward area to back area as follows - Batt HQ to LUCHEUX, "A" Coy to La Fontaine Fme, "B" Coy Lartbret, Bailleulmont "C" Coy to LARBRET D Coy to La Folie Fme. "A" & "D" Coys employed on Felling trees in LUCHEUX Forest & D Coy on Huts under O.C. Field Coys. "B" & "C" Coys working on Railway Embankment at CINCHON Valley & later employed on Railway Work. During month nothing to report other than above Coys employed on works as above.	
	22/1/17		A Coy moved to forward area "AGNY" for work under C.R.E. 30/IV.2	

H. Lemn
Lt. Colonel
Com'g 11th Staffs Regt (Pioneers).

11th (S) Bn. South Lancashire Regt.(Pioneers).

WAR   DIARY

of

the

11th (S) Bn. South Lancashire Reg.(Pioneers).

1st February, 1917   to   28th February, 1917.

VOLUME   16.

Army Form C. 2118

WAR DIARY
or
INTELLIGENCE SUMMARY

(Erase heading not required.)

Instructions regarding War Diaries and Intelligence Summaries are contained in F.S. Regs., Part II. and the Staff Manual respectively. Title Pages will be prepared in manuscript.

Place	Date	Hour	Summary of Events and Information	Remarks and references to Appendices
LUCHEUX	1917 1.2.		Disposition of Battalion. Bn. Hd.Qrs & Transport at LUCHEUX. "D" Coy at La Folie Farm. B & C Coys at LARBRET. "A" Coy in forward area at AGNY.	
	4.2.		Battalion (less "A" Coy at AGNY) moved to SIMENCOURT by march route via HUMBERCOURT - COUTERELLE SAULTY - BAVINCOURT - GOUY.	
	5.2		Battalion (less "A" Coy at AGNY) moved from SIMENCOURT to forward area as follows :- "D" Coy to ACHICOURT, "B" & "C" Coys to DAINVILLE Hd Qrs to DAINVILLE. Transport & Qr.Mr. Stores remained behind at SIMENCOURT, and later moved to MONCHIET (23rd Feby 1917)	
	27.2		"D" Coy moved from ACHICOURT to AGNY on 27th Feby 1917, the former village having passed to the 29th Division.	
			Companies employed during the period under review on the construction of Dugouts in the Line.	
			10 Casualties during month (all wounded).	
			Strength of Battalion on the 28th Feby 1917 :- 43 Officers 908 Other Ranks.	

C. Chamker Major for Lt.Col.(A.O.L.)
Comdg 11th S.Lancs Regt.(Pioneers).

CONFIDENTIAL.

WAR DIARY
OF
11th (S) Battn. SOUTH LANCASHIRE REGT.(PIONEERS)

from 1st March, 1917 to 31st March, 1917.

VOLUME No 17.

Army Form C. 2118

WAR DIARY
or
INTELLIGENCE SUMMARY
(Erase heading not required.)

Instructions regarding War Diaries and Intelligence Summaries are contained in F.S. Regs., Part II. and the Staff Manual respectively. Title Pages will be prepared in manuscript.

Place	Date	Hour	Summary of Events and Information	Remarks and references to Appendices
			From the beginning of the month until March 17th 1917 the Battalion was engaged in preparing dugouts, First Aid Posts and Collecting Stations in the forward trenches in front of AGNY.	
	18.3.17		First news of the enemy's retirement towards the COJEUL SWITCH LINE, which took place during the night, was received in the morning. All work was immediately stopped and the Battn stood to pending the arrival of fresh orders. These arrived at noon and A & B Coys went out from AGNY to the ARRAS-BUCQUOY the AGNY-BUCQUOY and the Mercatel SWITCH ROADS to prepare them for guns and transport. These roads behind the old German Lines had in several places been blown up. Temporary bridges were made round these spots while the craters were being filled in and on the ARRAS-BUCQUOY Road a very large concrete barrier which straggled it was removed. Several booby traps were discovered and rendered harmless. "C" & "B" Coys relieved A & B Coys during the night and the Battalion continued on the work in continuous shifts until the 22nd inst.	
	22.3.17.		Battalion marched to new Billeting area in BLAIRVILLE, which had been evacuated by the Germans. Before leaving they had blown up all buildings likely to provide shelter for our troops, but with the material strewn about the village the Battalion were soon able to provide accommodation for itself. Work was continued in making the roads passable for traffic where they had been blown up by the enemy.	

N. A. Fenn
Lt.Colonel.
Comdg 11th S. Lancs Regt.(Pioneers).

11th (S) Bn. South Lancashire Regt.(Pioneers).

WAR DIARY

of the

11th (S) Bn. South Lancashire Regiment. (Pioneers).

from

1st April, 1917 to 30th April, 1917

(VOLUME No. 18).

Army Form C. 2118

WAR DIARY
or
INTELLIGENCE SUMMARY
(Erase heading not required.)

Instructions regarding War Diaries and Intelligence Summaries are contained in F.S. Regs., Part II. and the Staff Manual respectively. Title Pages will be prepared in manuscript.

Place	Date	Hour	Summary of Events and Information	Remarks and references to Appendices
BLAIRVILLE.	1.4.		Battn. in Billets at BLAIRVILLE.	
	8.4.		From 1st April, 1917 to this date Battalion engaged on roads in vicinity of BOISLEUX St.MARC BOISLEUX au MONT BOIRY BECQUERELLE and ARRAS-BUCQUOY Rd, making them suitable for Lorry Traffic.	
	9.4.		Coys stand to and await orders to move on the most forward roads in connection with the offensive which commenced on this date.	
			At 3 p.m. "D" & "G" Coys moved off from Camp to commence work on the roads which detailed to them through Operation Order issued on the 7th.	
			"D" Coy cleared the MERCATEL - NEUVILLE VITASSE Road for Horse Traffic by 5 a.m. on the 10th. This road was used by lorries before dawn on the 11th.	
			"G" Coy went out to open for wheeled traffic Road running from BOIRY BECQUERELLE at T7.a.9.8 via Cross roads at T1.c.7.2. HENIN sur COJEUL MARTIN sur COJEUL, HENINEL WANCOURT, but owing to the unfavourable situation reports received, this Company was unable to work as far as detailed above. They worked on the HENIN - ST.MARTIN Road, which was opened for Horse Transport by the morning of the 11th April.1917.	
			At 6-30 a.m. on the 10th "A" Coy went out to work in relief of "D" Coy and "B" Coy in relief of "G" Coy.	
			The Arras-BAPAUME Road was reconnoitred and reported on during the 9th April.1917.	
			From morning of the 11th until the Battalion was relieved on the 13th work was carried on, on the forward roads. The work consisting chiefly in making the roads passable for lorries	

Army Form C. 2118

WAR DIARY
or
INTELLIGENCE SUMMARY

(Erase heading not required.)

Instructions regarding War Diaries and Intelligence Summaries are contained in F. S. Regs., Part II. and the Staff Manual respectively. Title Pages will be prepared in manuscript.

Place	Date	Hour	Summary of Events and Information	Remarks and references to Appendices
	12.4.	5 p.m.	The Battalion left BLAIRVILLE and marched to BASSEUX - BAILLEULMONT area.	
	13.4.		Moved back to St.AMAND, arriving there about 2 p.m. At about 11-30 p.m. however, Wire was received from the Division that XVIII Corps orders were that we should be lent to the VII Corps for work on roads, and that we were to march to BOISIEUX au Mont on the 14th. We arrived there about 3-30 p.m. on the 14th and the men finding there was no accommodation readily adapted themselves to the circumstances and speedily erected improvised shelters from material at hand.	
	14.4.			
	15.4.		Coys went out to work on roads in vicinity of BOISIEUX St.MARC and HENIN.	
	19.4.		Received orders from Division that we were to rejoin them on the 19th inst in the vicinity of BEAURAINS.	
	20.4.		On the morning of the 20th Coys went out to work on roads in the HENIN St MARTIN, HENINEL & NEUVILLE VITASSE areas.	
	23.4.		The work set out for the Battn in the operations which began upon the morning of April 23rd consisted in making the forward roads passable for artillery and transport. Later in the day as the result of certain developments in the situation one and half platoons companies were called out to hold positions in the Corps Defensive Line and two platoons companies formed a protective guard for a battery when the position of affairs appeared for a time to be precarious. "C" Coy paraded at 4-30 a.m. and were working on HENIN ST MARTIN HENINEL Rd towards CHERISY. They were working on this road up to the outskirts of HENINEL at 6 a.m. "B" Coy followed up two or three hours later with the intention of working on the other side of HENINEL towards CHERISY. Officers were sent forward to reconnoitre, but the situation throughout the morning appeared to be rather uncertain. The enemy shelled HENINEL very heavily and "C" Coy were quite unable to work in that village. "B" Coy found the road from HENINEL towards CHERISY also under very heavy fire. Consequently the two Coys collaborated on the road behind HENINEL and did much useful work, repairing it as far up as possible. "A" Coy also encountered lively shelling on their road which ran northwards out of HENINEL	

Army Form C. 2118

WAR DIARY
or
INTELLIGENCE SUMMARY
(Erase heading not required.)

Instructions regarding War Diaries and Intelligence Summaries are contained in F.S. Regs., Part II. and the Staff Manual respectively. Title Pages will be prepared in manuscript.

Place	Date	Hour	Summary of Events and Information	Remarks and references to Appendices
			Village. It was little more than a cart track; the Germans; the Germans had dug into its bank before it had been used, a short while previously, a part of our front line. The Coy managed to make it passable for transport before they ceased work on it.	
			By the end of the afternoon C & E Coys reported that the HENIN-ST.MARTIN-HENINEL Rd was open for Lorry traffic as far as the lastnamed village. In the evening two platoons of "D" Coy were sent out to endeavour to work beyond HENINEL towards CHERISY and arrived at the Reserve Line just as the Infantry were going over again. Here they remained for a short while and were just moving up to their task when, the O.C. of a battery requested their protection for his guns. This was immediately given, one platoon digging themselves in 200 yds in advance of the Battery and one in line with the guns. After a few hours when the situation had cleared up these two platoons proceeded to their original task and worked on the road between HENINEL and CHERISY.	
			"B" & "C" Coys had returned to camp and the men had just turned in when orders were received for a company to be sent to occupy two strong points in the Corps Defensive line. The effort and extent of the German counter attack on the right seemed to be doubtful and was the cause of this request. "B" Coy were speedily called out again and with two platoons of "D" Coy were sent off with two Lewis guns to occupy the two strong points. Here the men remained until relieved by the 90th Bde on the afternoon of the 24th.	
			On the following days, the Battalion continued the work on the roads around HENINEL.	
	28.4.		Battalion entrained at ARRAS Station and moved by train to Station about 8 miles S of St.POL. Marched to present Billets in BEAUVOIS.	

H. Fenn
Lt.Colonel.
Comdg 11th S.Lancs Regt.(Pioneers).

11th (S) Battn. South Lancashire Regt.(Pioneers).

WAR   DIARY
OF   THE
11th (S) Bn. S.Lancashire Regt.(Pioneers).

from 1st May,1917 to 31st May,1917.

(VOLUME 19)

Army Form C. 2118

WAR DIARY
or
INTELLIGENCE SUMMARY
(Erase heading not required.)

Place	Date	Hour	Summary of Events and Information	Remarks and references to Appendices
	1917		At the beginning of the month the Battalion was at BEAUVOIS, near ST.POL. It was the first time for many months that the battalion as a whole had been able to go into training and some useful work was done. On the 15th, a move was made to the adjoining village of OEUF. The Battalion did not stay here long, and, two days later it proceeded northwards by Bus staying on successive nights at ST.HILAIRE, HAZEBROUCK and PATRICIA CAMP Nr. POPERINGHE. From here it marched on the 20th to PALACE CAMP, near DICKEBUSCH. On the following day work was begun under the Chief Engineer Xth Corps upon Corduroy roads and Light railways. On the nights of the 27th, 28th and 29th PALACE CAMP was shelled by the enemy. Upon the 30th Division coming into the area the Battalion rejoined it, and on the night of the 31st marched to the ECOLE, East of YPRES, where it took up its quarters.	

W.F. Fenn
Lieut.Colonel.
Comdg. 11th S.Lancs Regt.(Pioneers).

11th (S) BATTN. SOUTH LANCASHIRE REGT. (PIONEERS).

CONFIDENTIAL.

W A R D I A R Y
O F
11th(S) Bn. South Lancashire Regt. (Pioneers).

From 1st June, 1917 to 30th June, 1917.

VOLUME 21.

WAR DIARY
or
INTELLIGENCE SUMMARY

(Erase heading not required.)

Army Form C. 2118

Place	Date 1917	Hour	Summary of Events and Information	Remarks and references to Appendices
YPRES. June.			At the beginning of the month the Battalion occupied the ECOLE to the East of YPRES, where it had arrived upon the 31st May,1917. Upon the night of the 3rd/4th June,1917, the whole Battalion was engaged in constructing a new fire trench 700 yards long, sited a distance of approximately 500 yards ahead of the front line. The trench, which ran South East of the MENIN Road, was to be 3ft wide & 3ft deep and it was arranged that the fire bays only should be dug, the traverses to be dug later. completed

The Battalion paraded 720 strong and the population of No Man's Land that night was increased by a wiring party furnished by the Field Coy R.E., and a covering party provided by the the 2nd Bedfordshire Regt. and the 19th King's Liverpool Regt.

The first Company started on the work at 11-10 p.m. but the company on the right, which was considerably delayed in reaching its task, did not begin much before midnight. Nevertheless by 1 o'clock the Coys had completed all the 77 fire bays together with the two strong points required. As it was at that time the enemy was fairly quiet, orders were issued for the Coys to begin work on the traverses.
During the whole night the enemy had been shelling fairly heavily a similar trench constructed shortly before on the left, later in the night they either saw or suspected that we were continuing it further south, because there was considerable machine gun fire, all of which went high, while 50 or 60 Shrapnel & H.E. shells were sent over. However, the only casualty on the work was one man wounded, and before the men were withdrawn at 2 a.m. 24 traverses had been completed and all the others were well under way.
When returning to the ECOLE the Battalion ran into a very heavy barrage of Gas shells which also covered the billets. Although Small Box Respirators were used two officers & 12 men were gassed and several others killed and wounded.
The M.O. did not consider it advisable for the men to work during the next 24 hours as so many were suffering from the effects of the gas. Upon the night of the 6th, however, the fire trench was completed and a communication trench back to the original front line was dug. Congratulatory messages upon the fire trench were received from the Divisional General and the C.R.E.
Work on the following nights was continued on trenches and roads. Upon 2 day of the Battle of MESSINES, the 30th Division being to the left of the attacking Army, this Battalion stood-to in anticipation of work being required upon the Divisional front.
The Battalion remained at the ECOLE until 13th. During that time it was every day very heavily shelled with Gas or H.E. and the larger portion of the heavy casualties suffered by the Battn | |

WAR DIARY
or
INTELLIGENCE SUMMARY

(Erase heading not required.)

Army Form C. 2118

Place	Date	Hour	Summary of Events and Information	Remarks and references to Appendices
			were sustained in Billets. On the night of the 13th the Battalion moved to the Railway Embankments Dugouts where it was hoped more rest for the men would be possible. This unhappily was not the case. Every day the quarters were shelled with Shrapnel and heavy calibre shells and between the 13th and 27th fifteen dugouts were smashed in. Gas Shells also were sent over on two nights.	
			Since the 13th one Company had occupied bivouacs & shelters near the CHATEAU SEGARD and on the 27th the remaining three companies moved to the same spot. This neighbourhood owing probably to the proximity of batteries soon developed signs of unhealthiness. Meanwhile the Companies had been working on VINCE ST. WELLINGTON CRESCENT. ZILLEBEKE ST & roads in the area which were under close observation by day and were invariably shelled at night. Their most important task was the construction of Four Assembly Trenches, since christened FENN Lane, RIDGE St, NORMAN St and KITE St together with one Communication trench joining them up & running from RITZ St to WELLINGTON Crescent. A Com. Tch were also dug running up VINCE ST with GOUROCK Rd about 270 yds long a trench boarded.	
			During the month of June,1917 the Battalion suffered a very large number of casualties 1 Officer being Killed, 1 Wounded and Died of Wounds later, and 3 Other Officers wounded, one of whom is still at duty. Other Ranks Killed 17, Wounded 88, Wounded still duty 38. These figures do not include Gas cases or Shell Shock cases.	

C. Chumpus Major. for Lt.Col.(A.O.L.)
Comdg.11th S.Lancs Regt.(Pioneers).

C O N F I D E N T I A L.

W A R D I A R Y

of the

11th(S) Bn. SOUTH LANCASHIRE REGIMENT.(PIONEERS).

1st JULY, 1917 to 31st JULY, 1917.

(VOLUME No. 22.)

Army Form C. 2118

WAR DIARY or INTELLIGENCE SUMMARY

(Erase heading not required.)

Instructions regarding War Diaries and Intelligence Summaries are contained in F. S. Regs., Part II. and the Staff Manual respectively. Title Pages will be prepared in manuscript.

Place	Date 1917	Hour	Summary of Events and Information	Remarks and references to Appendices
	1.7.		At the beginning of the month the Battalion occupied dugouts and shelters in the CHAU SEGARD Area. Practically all the work done was in preparation for the Operations which were to open at the end of the month. It consisted of the construction and upkeep of forward trenches, the making and maintenance of tracks, and the repair of roads damaged by Shell fire. Communication trenches were constructed between RITZ STREET and WELLINGTON CRESCENT - passing through Assembly Trenches built the previous month by the Battalion - and between VINCE ST & GOUROCK STREET. The activity of the enemy made maintenance parties upon VINCE ST. and the Trenches North and South of ZILLEBEKE LAKE a constant necessity. Roads which also required continual attention were the OBSERVATORY RIDGE ROAD & the SHRAPNEL CORNER-ZILLEBEKE ROAD.	
	13.7.		On the 13th "A" Company left the Battalion and the area, for the remainder of the month to work under the direction of the A.D.L.R. Fifth Army.	
	31.7.		Details of work &c on 31st July,1917 on sheet attached. Casualties during the month. Officers. Wounded. 2nd Lieut R J Struthers, 2nd Lieut R.L. Leake; Wounded Still duty, 2nd Lieut. W.J.Owen; 2nd Lieut. S.T.E. Clench. Other Ranks. Killed 6. Wounded. 76 (2 of which have since D of Wounds) Wounded,Still duty 17. The following N.C.O. and two men awarded the Military Medal for conspicuous gallantry No.20567 L/Cpl BLAKE W. 20842 Pte Orford J. No.21825 Pte Simpson J. No. 21450 4/Cpl. Saxon N. 21965 Pte Robinson J.V.	

C.C.Thompson Lt.Colonel.

Comdg.11th S.Lancs Regt.(Pioneers).

11th (S) Bn. South Lancashire Regt.(Pioneers).

WORK OF THE BATTALION on ZERO DAY (31st July, 1917).

The Work of the Battalion on ZERO DAY, allotted to the Battalion - less the 1 Company employed under the A.D.L.R.- consisted of opening up tracks to captured territory for the passage of guns and transport, and of constructing strong points, in conjunction with the R.E.s, a short distance behind the new British Front Lines.

Under ordinary weather conditions the actual task of making fresh tracks and maintaining the old ones would have produced no unsurmountable difficulties. To lay out "Fine Weather Tracks" in torrential rain proved to be quite another proposition. Very quickly the tracks became little more than quagmires, and work upon them had to be confined to pegging them out, clearing them of barbed wire and other obstacles and filling in or bridging old trenches. A shortage of hard material for filling in the shell holes & trenches added to the difficulties. Furthermore the parties working were shelled persistently.

"B" Company were engaged on the Artillery Track from OBSERVATORY RIDGE ROAD to STIRLING CASTLE. They left Chau Segard Area 1 hour after Zero. Everything was done to drain the track and to find wood etc. with which to fill in holes, but along it mud was over the boot tops. However by 7 p.m. the way was open for Light Guns as far as the old German Front Line. Owing to the activity of the enemy's Machine guns and snipers, attempts in daylight to work beyond the ridge - which was continuously shelled - had to be abandoned.
In the evening "C" Coy which had been in Divisional Reserve continued work on the Track. Orders were received to carry it as far forward as possible as a Track for Mules and to divert it under the ridge out of view in order to escape the heavy shelling. This was done. "B" Coy spent the night in trenches near the Work, and, with the assistance of "C" Coy carried on with the track during the next day. Both coys returned to Camp, the following evening.
Casualties were 1 Officer, wounded, Other Ranks killed one, Wounded 30.

1 Platoon of "D" Coy which set out before Zero, from Chau Segard was engaged on an Artillery track from ZILLEBEKE to I.24.a.8.8 and back. Similar difficulties to those fremupon the track mentioned above were encountered, but this track was successfully opened and maintained and was early in use by the Artillery.
Casualties. Other Ranks Killed one, Wounded nine.

3 Platoons of "D" Coy were engaged with part of 200th Field Coy R.E. in constructing Strong Points. This party remained "Standing to" in Zillebeke Street from 7-30 a.m. to 8 p.m. during which time there was very heavy shelling. At 8 p.m. instructions were received to proceed forward and to make 3 strong points just behind the "Blue Line". These were successfully completed, in face of exceptionally adverse conditions.
Casualties. Other Ranks Wounded 18, Wounded & Returned to duty 2.

Since the particular tasks allotted to the Battalion for ZERO day and Zero day plus one, work has consisted of the maintenance of these Tracks and Tracks Nos. 10 and 11 in addition. The only exception was on the night of August 2nd when 50 men worked with 200th Field Coy R.E. on wiring the new British Front Line for a distance of 900 yards. Casualties. NIL.

Upon Zero day and upon August 2nd South Lancs Transport provided men and Pack Animals for conveying R E Material to the line. Several animals were killed. On Zero day, one pack mule leader was wounded; On August 2nd one was killed and two wounded.

C.C.Champion Lt.Colonel.

9th Augst.1917.   Comdg.11th S.Lancs Regt.(Pioneers).

CONFIDENTIAL.

WAR DIARY

OF THE

11th (S) Bn. S. Lancashire Regt.(PIONEERS).

from 1st AUGUST,1917 to 31st AUGUST,1917.

VOLUME No. 23.

Army Form C. 2118

WAR DIARY
or
INTELLIGENCE SUMMARY
(Erase heading not required.)

Instructions regarding War Diaries and Intelligence Summaries are contained in F.S. Regs, Part II. and the Staff Manual respectively. Title Pages will be prepared in manuscript.

Place	Date	Hour	Summary of Events and Information	Remarks and references to Appendices
In the Field.	1917 August		At the beginning of the month the Battn was still in the CHATEAU SEGARD Area, S. of YPRES. Work was done upon forward Tracks and between the 1st & the 6th when the Battn. left the area, the casualties were 1 O.R. Killed and 15 O.R. wounded.	
			Upon the 5th the Battn marched to RENINGHELST Stn and entrained for GODEWAERSVELDE. Here it stayed until the 7th, when it marched to STRAZEELE & remained under canvas in the training area until the 11th inst. On that date the Battn marched and to EPSOM CAMP, Nr. Westoutre and began training. On the 16th however the Battn moved by road to VIERSTRAAT where work was begun upon the MESSINES RIDGE DEFENCES.	
			Upon the 16th 22nd inst. the Battalion moved from VIERSTRAAT to SPY FARM, Nr. LINLENHOEK taking over its present quarters from the Pioneers of the 4th Australian Divn. Work was done upon MANCHESTER ST (Forward C.T.), forward roads and camouflage.	
			The casualties between the 8th and the end of the month were two O.R.s wounded, making a total of oa 1 O.R. Killed and 17 O.R.s wounded during the month.	
			C Champion Lt.Colonel. Comdg. 11th S. Lancs Regt. (Pioneers).	

CONFIDENTIAL.

WAR DIARY

of

11th (S) Bn. South Lancashire Regt.,
(Pioneers).

from 1st September to 30th Sept. 1917

VOLUME 24.

Army Form C. 2118

WAR DIARY
or
INTELLIGENCE SUMMARY
(Erase heading not required.)

Instructions regarding War Diaries and Intelligence Summaries are contained in F.S. Regs., Part II. and the Staff Manual respectively. Title Pages will be prepared in manuscript.

Place	Date	Hour	Summary of Events and Information	Remarks and references to Appendices
In the Field.	1917 Sept.		At the beginning of the month the Battalion was still in the Camp taken over on the 22nd of August,1917 from the 4th Australian Division Pioneers. (SPY FARM Nr. LINDENHOEK). Work was continued during the month upon MANCHESTER ST (Forward C.T.) forward roads, camouflage, and from the 13th a Company & half employed on the erection of NISSEN HUTS in the vicinity of KEMMEL, also from the 17th inst. 1 Plato on engaged in the preparation of Winter Quarters for th a portion of the Battalion. During the month the total casualties were 10 Other Ranks wounded, 1 of whom Died.	

C.C.Champion

Lt.Colonel.
Comdg.11th S.Lancs Reg.(Pioneers).

CONFIDENTIAL.
................:O:.............

W A R ; O ; D I A R Y

o f

11th (S) Battn. South Lancashire Regt.(Pioneers).

from

1st OCTOBER, 1917   to   31st OCTOBER, 1917.

(VOLUME. 25.)

:0:0:0:0:0:0:0:0:0:

Army Form C. 2118

WAR DIARY
or
INTELLIGENCE SUMMARY
(Erase heading not required.)

Instructions regarding War Diaries and Intelligence Summaries are contained in F.S. Regs., Part II. and the Staff Manual respectively. Title Pages will be prepared in manuscript.

Place	Date	Hour	Summary of Events and Information	Remarks and references to Appendices
SPY FARM Nr. KEMMEL.	1917. Octr.		The Battalion was still at SPY FARM, the camp taken over on the 22nd August, 1917 from the 4th Australian Division Pioneers. Work was continued on Manchester St (Forward C.T.) until the 30th/31st Octr., on which date the trench was finished. Work was commenced the following night on DORSET ST. and BOB ST. Communication Trenches. During the month work was also carried out on the Roads in the Divisional Area, by 1 Company, 1 Company on NISSEN HUTMENTS in the vicinity of KEMMEL, and 1 Company on the preparation of WINTER QUARTERS at N.24.c.4.5., and work on SCREENS in Div. Area. Half Company also employed on the construction and laying of a Tramline in the forward area, running from In.De Sterke Cabaret O.15.a.3.2., to RAVINE O.10.d.10.70.	
			On the night 26/27th Octr. 1917, 2nd Lieut. J. Holmes, and 5 Other Ranks went out on Patrol from Post No.13 at O.17.central for the purpose of reconnoitreing an enemy Post at BANG FARM and its vicinity. Patrol left Post.13 at 12-30 a.m. and continued a parrallel route to VERNE Road until they reached the German Wire, which runs N & S and parallel to the Low Fm - Bang Fm Road and about 20 yards on the West side of the road. Wire only a few strands on Screw Pickets and easily passable. No actual gaps however were found in the wire. The ground west of Bang Fm. was found to be in good condition. When patrol approached enemy wire 6 Germans were observed carrying material which they dumped at O.17.b.90.25 and 25 yards from patrol. They commenced to dig in very muddy ground near the hedge. 2 of the enemy remained on Sentry, but as Patrol orders were to remain obtain information only, they remained stationary and later examined the trenches in the vicinity, all of which were found to be-go have fallen in, and apparently disused.	
			On the night of the 27/28th Oct. 1917, Lieut: W.J. Owen and 5 Other Ranks went out on Patrol from Post No.13 for the purpose of reconnoitring the Post mentioned above, but on this occasion patrol only reached a point near VERNE Road at O.17.b.25.10 where an enemy working party was observed 30 yards ahead. At O.17.c.45.10 across the VERNE Road is a double belt of concertina barbed wire, each belt 3 yards apart and each 50 ft in length and which appears to be a road barricade only.	

WAR DIARY
or
INTELLIGENCE SUMMARY
(Erase heading not required.)

Army Form C. 2118

Place	Date	Hour	Summary of Events and Information	Remarks and references to Appendices
			On the 28th/29th Octr.1917 a Patrol consisting of 2nd Lieut. J.Holmes, 1 Warrant Officer and 9 Other Ranks, went out from No.13 Post at O.17.central at 11-45 p.m. for the purpose of continuing reconnaisance of BANG FARM, and if possible to secure a prisoner. When Patrol had proceeded 20 yards past our own wire, an enemy party of 15 to 20 strong was observed walking to and fro' from O.17.b.63.15 on the VERNE ROAD to the opposite hedge at O.17.b.60.32. The Patrol Leader and a N.C.O. advanced to within close view of this party, at the same time protecting their flanks with the remainder of the patrol. As the enemy party considerably outnumbered our Patrol, nothing could be done at the moment other than wait developments. From the noise of the Iron Pickets being used and pairs of the enemy halting at each Piket, it was obvious that the enemy was wiring. They continued this work for a hour and a quarter. The enemy party was protected by 3 groups of double sentries behind trees on the VERNE Road, each group being 20 yards apart and held connection by occasional patrols between each group.

During the month one man was slightly wounded by an ~~enemy~~ aeroplane dud shell, but remained at duty. | |

Comdg.11th S. Lancs Regt.(Pioneers). Lt.Colonel.

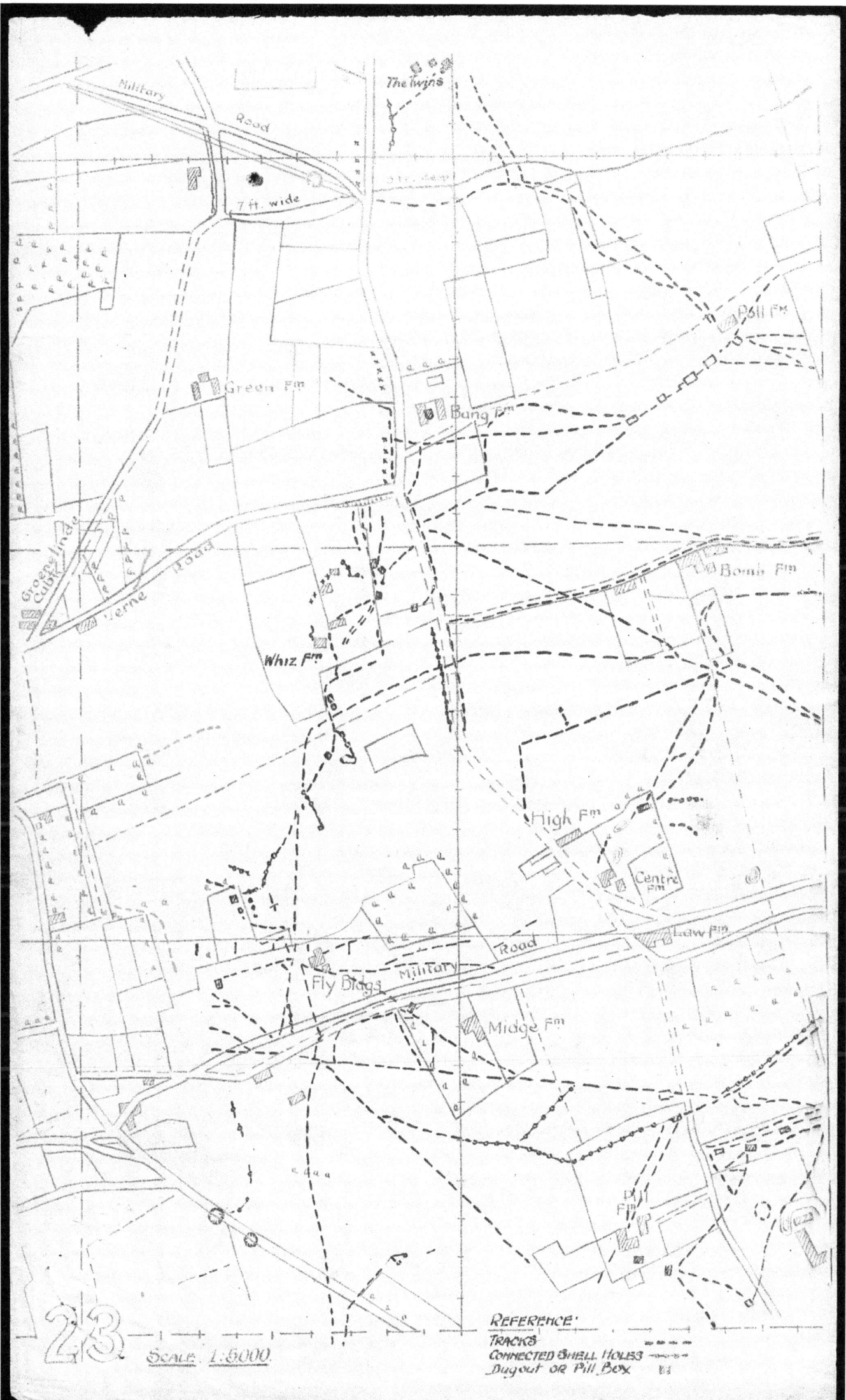

CONFIDENTIAL.

WAR DIARY

of the

11th (S) Bn. South Lancashire Regiment. (Pioneers).

from

1st November, 1917 to 30th November, 1917.

(VOLUME No. 26).

xxxxxxxxxxx

Army Form C. 2118

WAR DIARY
or
INTELLIGENCE SUMMARY

(Erase heading not required.)

Instructions regarding War Diaries and Intelligence Summaries are contained in F. S. Regs., Part II. and the Staff Manual respectively. Title Pages will be prepared in manuscript.

Place	Date	Hour	Summary of Events and Information	Remarks and references to Appendices
SPY FARM	1.11.		The Battalion was still at Spy Farm in the same camp as taken over from the 4th Aust. Division Pioneers on the 22nd August 1917. Work was continued on DORSET & BOB ST. Communication Trenches NISSEN HUTS were constructed in the vicinity of KEMMEL for Brigade in Reserve. Tramway Line was laid in the forward area, running from In de Sterke Cabaret 0.15.a.3.2. to the RAVINE 0.10.d.10.70. All roads in the forward Divisional Area were repaired and maintained. Work done on all screens in the Divisional Area. Winter Quarters for the Battalion were continued with at N.24.c.4.5.	
			The foregoing work was carried on by the Battalion until the 8th Nov. 1917 when orders were received from the Division for the Battalion to be prepared to move on the following morning to BAILLEUL. On the 9th November, we were relieved by the 5th Australian Pioneer Battn. who took over SPY FARM Camp, and all work in the Divisional Area which the Battalion had been employed on. On the 11th inst Battalion moved by BUS from BAILLEUL to YPRES (S.W.) On the 13th inst. the Battalion was ordered to move to Salvation Corner N.W. of YPRES and took over the Camp of the 2nd Bn. Canadian Pioneers. On the 14th inst the Battalion was employed on forward roads in the Passchendale Sector, &c. in order to get these roads open for and repaired for Field Artillery &c. for a contemplated operation. On the 24th inst. orders were received for the Battalion to move to I.31.d.5.5.(Sheet 28) Nr. VORMEZEELE, and take over the camp and work from the 13th Gloucestershire Regt. Owing to the urgency of the opening and clearing of the ST.JEAN-BELLEVUE Road, two Coys were ordered to remain behind to complete this work, and join Battalion on the 25th at I.31.d.5.5. All work was taken over from the Gloucestershire Regt. and consisted of work on PERTH AVENUE C.T., and construction and maintenance of all Plankroads, Mule Tracks and Infantry Duckboard tracks. On 26th November, orders were received to move two Coys to ZILLEBEKE BUND, 29th 1 Coy to ZILLEBEKE BUND, and on 30th remaining Coy to RAILWAY DUGOUTS. Battn Hd.Qrs & details moved to ZILLEBEKE BUND on 1st December,1917. On and from 26th November,1917 the Battalion work was re-arranged and more work taken on which included 1 Coy under orders of G.O.C. Brigade in Line, 1 Coy under orders of Field Coy R.E. in Line on Supporting Points.	
			Casualties incurred during the month were Other Ranks Killed 1, Wounded 9, Wounded,still duty 8.	

H. Penn Lt.Colonel.
Comdg.11th S. Lancs Reg.(Pioneers).

CONFIDENTIAL.

WAR DIARY

of

the

11th (S) Bn. South Lancashire Regt. (Pioneers).

1st December, 1917 to 31st December, 1917.

Army Form C. 2118

WAR DIARY
or
INTELLIGENCE SUMMARY

(Erase heading not required.)

Instructions regarding War Diaries and Intelligence Summaries are contained in F.S. Regs., Part II. and the Staff Manual respectively. Title Pages will be prepared in manuscript.

Place	Date 1917	Hour	Summary of Events and Information	Remarks and references to Appendices
ZILLEBEKE BUND.	1.12		Battalion Hd.Qrs. and Coys still in Dugouts at ZILLEBEKE BUND. 1 Coy in Dugouts (RAILWAY) Disposition the same as reported in last War Diary for November,1917.	
			Work carried on during the month of December as under -	
			1 Company on Tracks (Infantry Duckboard Tracks). 1 Company on Mule Tracks. 1 Company under the orders of G.O.C. Brigade in Left Sector. 1 Company under orders of O.C. Field Coy R.E. in Line.	
			2nd Lieut. Holman A.E. and 2nd Lieut. J.J. Aston wounded during December,1917. Other Ranks - Killed 4, Wounded 8.	
			Sergt. T. Smart, L/Cpl. Bishop J. & Pte. Prescott W awarded Military Medal for Gallantry in Action, in the Field.	
			[signature] Lt.Colonel.	
			Comdg. 11th S.Lancs Regt. (Pioneers).	

CONFIDENTIAL

WAR DIARY

of

11th (S) Battalion, South Lancashire Regt.,
(Pioneers).

from

1st January, 1918

to

31st January, 1918.

. . . .

(VOLUME 28.)

Army Form C. 2118.

WAR DIARY
or
INTELLIGENCE SUMMARY.
(Erase heading not required.)

Instructions regarding War Diaries and Intelligence Summaries are contained in F.S. Regs., Part II. and the Staff Manual respectively. Title pages will be prepared in manuscript.

Place	Date	Hour	Summary of Events and Information	Remarks and references to Appendices
	1918. Jan.1		At the beginning of the month the Battalion occupied Dugouts at ZILLEBEKE BUND (B.H.Q. & 3 Coys) and RAILWAY DUGOUTS (1 Coy). Regtl Transport & Q.M. details billeted at DICKEBUSCH.	
	" 4		Regimental Transport moved from DICKEBUSCH by march route to RACQUINGHAM, arriving there in the evening of the 5th January. Battalion moved on the 5th instant to RACQUINGHAM, proceeding by rail from DICKEBUSCH.	
	" 8		Battalion and Regtl Transport moved from RACQUINGHAM to AMIENS area, marching to STEENBECQUE from where the Battalion entrained. On arrival at detraining station, LONGEAU, Battalion marched to new area and billeted as follows:- B.H.Q. BLANGY TRONVILLE CHATEAU. 2 Coys GLISSY 2 Coys BLANGY. Until the 12th inst. time spent in training.	
	" 13		On the 13th Jany.1918 the Battalion and Transport proceeded to PROYART by march route, a distance of 15 miles.	
	" 14		On the 14th Jany 1918 the Battalion and Transport marched from PROYART to CURCHY & ETALON area, B.H.Q. and 2 Coys being billeted at CURCHY and 2 Coys at ETALON. On the evening of the same date orders received for 2 Coys to move to OFFOY (3 miles W of HAM.) on the following morning by march route for attachment to XVIII Corps. The remaining 2 Coys (C & D) billeted with B.H.Q. at CURCHY carried on with Training until the 18th inst when orders were received that Battalion, less the 2 Coys detached, would move the following day to NESLE for work under the orders of C.R.E. 5th Army Troops.	
	" 20.		Work commenced on the renovation of Billets &c preparatory to the 5th Army Headquarters arriving in NESLE.	
	" 22.		1 Officer and 50 Other Ranks proceeded by Motor Lorries to BONNEUIL CHATEAU for work on HANGARS and mens Huts.	
	" 25.		1 Officer and 6 Lewis Gun Teams with Guns proceeded to VILLERS-ST-CHRISTOPHE and HAM for Anti-Aircraft protection, in accordance with orders received direct from XVIII Corps.	

Army Form C. 2118.

WAR DIARY
or
INTELLIGENCE SUMMARY.
(Erase heading not required.)

Place	Date	Hour	Summary of Events and Information	Remarks and references to Appendices
	1918. 31.1.		Final dispositions of Battalion on the 31st January, 1918:- 2 Coys located near ETREILLERS & GRAND SERAUCOURT for work under XVIII Corps. 2 Coys & Bn. Hd. Qrs at NESLE under orders of C.R.E. 5th Army Troops. 1 Officer & 50 men at BONNEUIL CHATEAU under orders of C.R.E. 5th Army Troops. 1 Officer & 6 Lewis Gun Sections at VILLERS-ST-CHRISTOPHE and HAM for A.A. protection. 2nd Lieut. Holman A.E. and 2nd Lieut. J.J. Acton returned from Hospital on the 21st & 24th insts having been wounded in December 1917. Other Ranks Wounded 2. Lieut. (Captain) A.G. DEAN awarded the Military Cross for Gallant Service in the Field London Gazette 3.1.1918. L/Sergt. Potter J. awarded the Distinguished Conduct Medal for gallant service in the Field London Gazette 5.1.1918. Total strength of Battalion on the 31.1.1918. 37 Officers and 869 Other Ranks. C. Champion Major for Lt.Colonel. (A.O.D.) Commanding 11th South Lancashire Regt. (Pioneers).	

CONFIDENTIAL

WAR DIARY

of

11th (S) Bn. South Lancashire Regt.
(Pioneers).

from

1st February 1918

to

28th February 1918.

....

VOLUME 29.

Army Form C. 2118.

WAR DIARY
or
INTELLIGENCE SUMMARY.
(Erase heading not required.)

Instructions regarding War Diaries and Intelligence Summaries are contained in F.S. Regs., Part II. and the Staff Manual respectively. Title pages will be prepared in manuscript.

Place	Date 1918	Hour	Summary of Events and Information	Remarks and references to Appendices
	Feby 1st.		At the beginning of the month the Battalion was located as reported in the last portion of the War Diary for the month of January, 1918.	
	" 13th		Work carried on as usual until the 13th Feby.1918, when orders were received that Bn. Hd. Qrs and 2 Coys would move from NESLE on the 14th Feby.1918 to destinations as under:- Hd. Qrs. to DURY - "C" Coy to ROUPY - "D" Coy to SAVY.	
	" 17th		In the meantime "C" & "D" Coys were employed on the improvement of their Billets, after which date, they were employed on work under the orders of O.C. Field Coys R.E. preparing Defence Lines.	
	" 20th		"A" Coy. 5 Platoons moved from ATILLY to DURY for the purpose of erecting NISSEN HUTS for the Divisional Headquarters who moved in to DURY on the 25th Feby.1918, remaining Platoon of "A" arrived at DURY on the 22nd inst. to assist in erection of NISSEN HUTS.	
	" 26th		On this date Bn. Hd. Qrs and Transport vacated Billets at DURY and moved to FLUQUIERES in the forward area, the 3 Platoons remaining behind at DURY for the purpose of finishing off erection of Nissen Huts and completing Billets. 1 Platoon of "A" Coy moved to AUBIGNY to erect NISSEN HUTS and Bunking Barns.	
	" 28th		One platoon moved from DURY to FLUQUIERES for the purpose of erecting NISSEN HUTS for R.A.	
	Mch 31st		A further platoon moved from DURY to FLUQUIERES for the purpose of erecting HUTS at VAUX.	
			The following is the final distribution of the Battalion on the 1st March 1918.	
			"A" Coy H.Q. and 1 Platoon at DURY. 1 Platoon at AUBIGNY and 2 Platoons at FLUQUIERES "B" Coy located at SAVY working under orders of 200th Field Coy R.E. in Forward Zone. "C" Coy located at ROUPY working under orders of 202nd Field Coy R.E. Bn BATTLE ZONE. "D" Coy located at A.8.a.(Sheet 66d N.E) under orders of 201st Field Coy R.E. working on REDOUBTS & KEEPS (Battle Zone).	
			No casualties suffered during the month of February 1918.	
			[signature] Lt.Colonel. Comdg.11th S. Lancs Regt.(Pioneers).	

Pioneers.
30th Div.

11th BATTN. THE SOUTH LANCASHIRE REGIMENT.

M A R C H

1 9 1 8

Attached:-

Report on Operations
21st/28th March.

CONFIDENTIAL

WAR DIARY

of

11th (S) Bn. South Lancashire Regt.,
(Pioneers). 30th RDW.

from
1st March 1918
to
31st March 1918.

VOLUME 30.

Army Form C. 2118.

WAR DIARY
or
INTELLIGENCE SUMMARY.
(Erase heading not required.)

Instructions regarding War Diaries and Intelligence Summaries are contained in F.S. Regs., Part II. and the Staff Manual respectively. Title pages will be prepared in manuscript.

Place	Date	Hour	Summary of Events and Information	Remarks and references to Appendices
March 1st	1918		At the beginning of the month the Battalion was located as reported in the last portion of the War Diary for the month of February 1918.	
			Work carried on on the Forward Zone, Battle Zone & Redoubts and Keeps in the SAVY - ROUPY Area. (N of ST. QUENTIN).	
	8.3.		On the 8th March 1918 the Battalion was reorganised from 4 Coys to 3 Coys in accordance with G.H.Q. instructions, consequently dispositions of Coys were changed and read as under :-	
			"A" Coy H.Q. and 1 Platoon at ROUPY. 1 Platoon at A.3.d. (Sheet 66c N.W.) 1 Platoon at AUBIGNY.	
			"B" Coy H.Q. and 4 Platoons remained at SAVY WOOD.	
			"C" Coy H.Q. and 3 Platoons remained at ROUPY. 1 Platoon at FLUQUIERES.	
	20.3.		Work was continued until the 20th inst (inclusive)	
	21.3.		Report on Operations from 21st to 28th March 1918 (inclusive) attached hereto.	
			Casualties incurred during the month as under :-	
			Officers - 2nd Lieut. J.P. Mallalieu, Wounded 21.3.18. 2/Lt. G. Thomson, Wounded. 23.3.18	
			Capt. H.A. Hodges. Missing believed Killed 22.3.18. 2/Lt. H.C. Harvey, Wounded. 23.3.18	
			Lieut. C.R. Featherby. Wounded 22.3.18. Lieut. N.S. Reamsbottom. 27.3.18	
			Lieut. J.C. Lidgett. Killed. 23.3.18. (Wounded).	
			2/Lt. A. Knight. Killed. 23.3.18. 2/Lt. A.E. Holman, Wounded 28.3.18	
			Lieut. S.W. McLeod-Braggins, Wounded. 28.3.18. 2/Lt. G.R. Tomkinson. " 28.3.18	
			Other Ranks. Killed. 14. Wounded 195. Wounded & Missing 5. Missing 194. (During Operations).	
			Other Ranks. Wounded 1 on the 17.3.1918.	
	30.3.		The Battalion entrained at SALEUX for VALERY-Sur-SOMME. On the 31st March Battalion located at LANCHERES, near VALERY-Sur-SOMME.	

M. Fenn
Lt. Colonel.
Comdg. 11th (S) Bn. South Lancashire Regt. (Pioneers).

11th. SOUTH LANCASHIRE REGT. (PIONEERS).

REPORT ON OPERATIONS FROM 21st. TO 28th. MARCH 1918 INCLUSIVE.

21st. On the morning of the 21st. my Battalion was situated as follows:-
   One Company at Savvy Wood Dugouts.
   One Company in Roupy.
   One Company split up between L'Epine de Dallon - Roupy and the back area.

In accordance with Divisional Defence Scheme, as soon as enemy artillery fire made it seem probable that an attack was imminent, all Companies proceeded to Fluquieres. The Company in Savvy Wood lost a certain number of men owing to the fact that the enemy put down a heavy barrage of Gas and H.E. Shells. A few men who were working with the R.Es. in L'Epine de Dallon did not get clear.

At 3 o'clock p.m. we were ordered to withdraw from Fluquieres to the quarry behind Aviation Wood. This was done and picquets were posted on the East side of Aviation Wood.

About 7.30 p.m. G.S.O. 3 30th. Division informed me that I was responsible for my own defence. I accordingly took up a line between Mill Wood and Aviation Wood running from F.25.B.3.2. - F.25.D.6.8. - to L.1.b.5.0. - L.1.D.3.2. This line was dug and partially wired.

22nd. I informed G.O.C. 21st. Brigade my position and received orders that I was to hold on to the position and if the infantry in front were compelled to withdraw, they would withdraw through me and reform behind.

The Battallion remained here, with picquets out in front of Aviation Wood and on each flank until 6 p.m. on the 22nd.

About that time two Companies of the 17th. Kings withdrew on to our line and were being placed into position to strengthen our line when orders were received that all troops were to withdraw in an orderly fashion on HAM. At the time we withdrew the enemy was just coming into view on the crest S.W. of Aviation Wood.

On arrival at Ham I received orders to bivouac at EPPEVILLE.

23rd. About 4.30 on the morning of the 23rd. a certain amount of enemy machine gun fire was heard. I received information from small Units of the 36th. Division, T.M. Batteries - R.Es. that everybody was retiring, the enemy was in Ham and that the R.Es. were waiting for the last troops to come through to blow up the bridge over the canal at K.32.b.1.7. (66 2)

I sent one Platoon as a covering party to the R.Es. at the bridge, 1 Platoon to my front to take up a position near the canal N. of Eppeville and one platoon on the left towards Canizy while the remainder of the Battalion had breakfast on the road.

As I had received no orders of any kind and did not know what was happening on either flank or even if it was intended to hold the line of the canal, I sent to the 89th. Brigade at Esmery Hallon for orders. I waited there until 7 a.m. during which time the canal bridge had been blown up and a considerable number of small units had withdrawn down the Ham-Eppeville Road. A number of men of the 23rd. Entrenching Battalion who stated that they were holding the front line also withdrew through us. I accordingly sent the Battalion under Major Champion along the Ham-Eppeville Road to wait at the cross roads at J.33.b.6.2. until I could get further information from the Brigade. Shortly after, I met the G.S.O. 1, 20th. Division in a car. I told him the situation as far as I knew it and he informed me that Canizy was being held and that the 30th. Division was supposed to hold the line of the canal. I brought the Battalion back and intended getting into trenches which I understood had been dug along the canal bank with my

1.

left on Ganizy and try and get into touch with somebody on my right.

The head of the Battalion had reached about J.35 Central when information was received from some men of the 19th. Kings that the enemy had crossed the canal and was coming on.

I then posted two Companies in some trenches on the high ground from about J.35.c. to about J.35.d.4.7., protecting the right flank and one Company on the Railway embankment from J.34.a.6. to J.34.b.4.1.

Men of the 19th. Kings under Capt. 5 th were in trenches from about J.34.b.5.1. to about J.35.c.7. . The 23rd. Entrenching Battalion were also holding trenches and part of the Railway towards Ganizy but for a considerable time I had no exact knowledge as to where they were.

I was not in touch with anyone on my right.

I then sent out a patrol to reconnoitre the Eppeville-Ham Road as far as the cross roads at K.31.b.8.0. This patrol reported no signs of the enemy. I accordingly sent out two companies to hold the line of the Railway from J.35.b.4.0. to J.36.c.3.7. with orders to send out a patrol to try and get in touch with someone on our right. About 10 a.m. I received information that the enemy appeared to be massing on the north of the canal and then until about 12.30 there was a considerable number of the enemy moving about in the wood J.29. and J.30. and fairly heavy rifle fire. The enemy appeared to have intended to attack but did not succeed in reaching our line.

About 2 p.m. the 182nd. Brigade was seen advancing from our left in the direction of Verlane. They informed me that they intended to attack Verlane, which I knew to be unoccupied by the enemy and to proceed in a north-easterly direction towards Ham.

Just previously, my right Company on the Railway Embankment observed the enemy advancing in a south-westerly direction on their right rear. As the Company Commander had failed to get in touch with anyone on his right and as the enemy was on three sides of him, both Companies withdrew to their former positions.

About 6 p.m. I met the O.C. 182nd. Brigade, the O.C. 23rd. Entrenching Battalion and the O.C. of a composite Battalion which was on the left of the 182nd. Brigade and we arranged to reorganize so as to hold a consecutive line. The O.C. Composite Battalion stated that he was holding a line with his left on the Sucrerie at K.31.a.5.2. It afterwards proved that he did not know where his line was and as a matter of fact his left was about 500 yards in rear of it. I arranged to get in touch with him with my right flank that night at the Sucrerie and with the 23rd. Entrenching Battalion on my left at J.35.b.4.0. Accordingly at 9.30 p.m. two companies took up a line on the Railway in touch with the 23rd. Entrenching Battalion on our left and the right Company Commander attempted to get in touch with the Composite Battalion at the Sucrerie which turned out to be held by the enemy and the Officer was either killed or captured. At the same time heavy enemy machine gun fire was directed on us from the right flank straight down the Railway line. The enemy also sent up the S.O.S. and turned his Artillery and Trench Mortars on to the Railway cutting. When things became quiet I went to the O.C. 182nd. Brigade and informed him what had happened.

24th.

The O.C. 23rd. Entrenching Battalion could not be found until 5 o'clock in the morning when he admitted that he had made a mistake as to his front line.

As it was then too late to dig a new line back to the Composite Battalion position and as my position would have been untenable in daylight, I arranged with the O.C. 182nd. Brigade to withdraw to my old position and to have some men in support in case the enemy came through the gap between our right and the Composite Battalion's left. About 7 a.m. on the 24th. the enemy commenced to shell our line. Soon after 8 a.m. I saw men of the 23rd. Entrenching Battalion withdrawing from the direction of Ganizy. I at once sent orders to the Company in reserve to come up but before they could get into position the troops were falling back on both flanks. The two Companies who were holding the line J.35.c. & d. were almost

2.

entirely surrounded, their only line of withdrawal was across the stream
in J.35.c. which was lined with barbed wire. Owing to the magnificent
way in which the Lewis Gunners remained firing at the enemy until they were
either killed or wounded, parts of the two Companies withdrew and fought
a rearguard action, across the canal near Moyencourt, where they held
trenches.

Meanwhile Battalion H.Qrs. were compelled to withdraw and
attempted to find the Company in reserve. This proved impossible
owing to the large number of scatted troops retiring. A number of
these were reformed and acted as a covering party to various batteries
in turn. When about 1 kilo. east of Libermont, I met General Goodman
who told me to take up a position there. This was held from 12 noon
until about 6.30 p.m. when I received orders to withdraw through the
French and take up a line in rear of the Division, between Moyencourt
and Crossy. On arrival I reported to the 189th. Brigade and was
ordered to hand over the men to their Units and report to Divisional
H.Qrs. The reserve Company had fought a rearguard action to Moyencourt when it joined up with the remainder of the Battalion.
Major Champion attempted to join up with the reserve Company on his
left but when about 100 yards from them discovered that it was the
enemy and not the reserve Company that he was approaching. The Companies were mixed up with other Units largely V.C.Vs. who retired in
a S.W. direction but fell back gradually towards Ramecourt. When a
little N.W. of Esmery Hallon, General Williams rode up. The enemy
were then nearly 1000 yards away and there was no difficulty in
stopping their advance straight ahead. Owing to troops on right or
left continually withdrawing, however, it was impossible to stay in
our position indefinitely. A battery was covered while it withdrew
(A 92) and a point level with Esmery Hallon held about 11 a.m.
Ramecourt bridge was crossed at 1 p.m., a Staff Captain riding out and
telling us to come back over the bridge. The Battalion was then
collected and reported to Lt.Col. Rollo who had command of the defences.
We were ordered to Roieglise about 10 p.m. getting there at 6 a.m. 25th.

25th.
On the 25th. Battalion withdrew to Roieglise. During the
day I was ordered to take command of a Divisional Composite Battalion.
At 5 p.m. the Composite Battalion was ordered to proceed to Plessier
where it was billeted at 1 a.m. 26th.

26th.
At 10 a.m. on the 26th. I was ordered to proceed with the Composite Batt. at once
to take up a line between Rouvray inclusive to le Quesnel returning
as many men as possible to their Units on the march. All men of
other Units were handed over. On arrival at the Rouvroy-Bouchoir
Road I met O.C. 89th. Brigade who ordered me to take up a line in
some old trenches with my left in front of Rouvroy and informed me
that the 19th. Kings would come in on my right when they arrived.
This was completed about 8 p.m. I was then in touch on my left with
a battalion of the Royal Warwickshire Regt.

Shortly after, the Warwicks withdrew from the line. I
reported to 89th. Brigade and 150 men of 17th. K.L.R. were sent to
hold the line in front of Rouvroy at about 8 p.m. At 11 p.m. O.C.
17th. K.L.R. reported they were in touch on their left.

As a number of old communication trenches ran back from
the enemy to my front line I had them filled in for 100 yards in front.

Patrols were sent out about 1000 yards in front and got
in touch with the enemy over the crest, at 4 p.m. Patrolling was
carried on all night.

27th.
At 9 a.m. on the 27th. men of the 17th. Kings commenced
to move to their right along my front line, they were ordered to
return to their trenches which they did. About 10 a.m. the 17th.
K.L.R. withdrew behind Rouvroy without informing me of their intention.

3.

I heard that the troops on their left had also withdrawn. I ordered my *left* Company to form a defensive flank and reported to the 89th. Brigade. I consulted with Lt.Col. Rollo and we decided that we could hold on but wanted supports sent up on our left as enemy snipers had by then occupied Rouvroy and were enfilading my trenches. At about 10.45 a.m. I received orders from Brigade by telephone to withdraw on a line Hangest Plessier. I understood that troops on right of Divisional line had also withdrawn.

The 19th. K.L.R. and 11th. South Lancs. then withdrew in extended order giving each *other* covering fire until they reached a point S. of Folies where they got into Artillery formation, and withdrew as far as the quarry on the Roye-Amiens Road, E. of Folies.

The rearguard again got into touch with the 17th. K.L.R. due N. of Rouvroy. The officer in charge was ordered by the Brigade Major 72nd. Brigade to hold on there, which he did until the 61st. Division had dug in just in rear of him. He then rejoined the Battalion, *at about 8 p.m.*

At the Quarry was met by a Colonel on horseback who said the withdrawal was due to a mistake. I then reformed my battalion into extended order and counter-attacked together with the 2nd. R.S.F. 2nd Bedfords, 19th. K.L.R., and a Battalion of Manchesters on the left.

We advanced to a line running in front of Folies and along road from Folies towards Arvillers, where we were held up by Machine Gun and Trench mortar fire from Arvillers and Bouchoir. We then occupied an old trench with a few men on the road in front. I there met Colonel Blore who told me to hold that line. I consulted with Colonel Kelso, R.S.F., and Major Synn of the Bedfords and as the trench was too packed with men, we decided to reorganize at dusk. Bedfords to hold the right in touch with R.Fs. on the Roye-Amiens Road, K.L.Rs. on left in touch with some Manchesters. South Lancs. to dig a support line 300 yards in rear with 19th. K.L.R. in reserve, already dug in 400 yards in rear again.

26th.

On the morning of the 28th. the enemy commenced to shell our positions, it became necessary to remove some of the men in the support line to the left flank.

At 11.30 a.m. the R.I.R. on the right flank withdrew under orders of an Officer of that Regiment. I sent one Company across the road to defend the flank. By 12.15 p.m. all R.I.R. on right flank had withdrawn. It became necessary to send all the 11th South Lancs, and some of the 19th. K.L.R. on to the flank in order to keep the enemy from debouching from Arvillers. This was successfully done. At 1.30 p.m. I was informed by 89th. Brigade that the French had relieved us and that we were to withdraw through them. I arranged with Col. Rollo and Col. Kelso that we would hold the flank until the troops in the front line had withdrawn. This was successfully accomplished.

The Battalion then withdrew to Rouvrel.

2.4.18.
Lieut.Col.
Comdg. 11th. South Lancashire Regt.(Pioneers)

CONFIDENTIAL.

WAR DIARY

of

11th (S) Bn. South Lancashire Regt.,
(Pioneers).

from

1st APRIL, 1918

to

30th APRIL, 1918.

VOLUME. 31.

Army Form C. 2118.

WAR DIARY
or
INTELLIGENCE SUMMARY.
(Erase heading not required.)

Instructions regarding War Diaries and Intelligence Summaries are contained in F.S. Regs., Part II. and the Staff Manual respectively. Title pages will be prepared in manuscript.

Place	Date 1918	Hour	Summary of Events and Information	Remarks and references to Appendices
Lanchieres	31.3		The Battalion located as reported in the last portion of the War Diary for the month of March 1918, viz. LANCHIERES, Nr. Valery-sur-Somme.	
"	5.4		At midnight the battalion marched to FOUQUIERES, there entraining at 6 a.m. and detraining at ROOSBURGGE at 9 p.m. From detraining station conveyed by Lorries to YORK CAMP, N.W. of Poperinghe.	
	7.4		Battalion marched from York Camp to TURCO CAMP, N.E. of YPRES (Sh.28/C.15.c) Transport located at OTTER CAMP A.12.a.l.5. (Sh.28) Battalion relieved the 1st Division Pioneer Battn. and took over work on Duckboard Tracks and Roads in front of the STEENBEEK and within the Divisional Boundaries.	
	10.4		On the 10.4.18 all Coys paraded as strong as possible for work on the wiring of the BATTLE ZONE.	
	11.4		1 Coy continued work on roads, 1 Coy work on Tracks, and 1 Coy work on Forward Posts.	
	16.4		Battalion moved to LOCHAEL CAMP (Sh.28. B.15.c.9.2.) Coys moving to this Camp after completion of work on Strong Points and Battle Zone area.	
	18.4		Battalion moved by march route under orders of 21st Inf. Brigade to Camp situated at G.23.c.6.4. Nr. RENINGHELST.	
	19.4		Coys working on Strong Points situated Nr. Ouderdom. 2nd Bn. Wilts Regt. assisted with work.	
	25.4		Work carried on, on the Strong Points situated Nr. Ouderdom until the 25.4.18 when Battalion was ordered to remain in Camp and be prepared to move at half hour's notice. No work was carried out on 25.4.18 due to the enemy heavy bombardment and subsequent attacks. At 3 p.m. received orders to move at once to LAWRENCE CAMP G.11.c.6.5. (Sh.28)	
	27.4.		Battalion attached to the C.R.E. 49th Division for work on and from 6 a.m. 27.4.18.	
	28.4.		Battalion moved to L.23.b.central (Sh. 27) and prepared camp for occupation, Coys joining B.H.Q. after completion of work on Forward roads that day.	

Army Form C. 2118.

WAR DIARY
or
INTELLIGENCE SUMMARY.
(Erase heading not required.)

Instructions regarding War Diaries and Intelligence Summaries are contained in F. S. Regs., Part II. and the Staff Manual respectively. Title pages will be prepared in manuscript.

Place	Date	Hour	Summary of Events and Information	Remarks and references to Appendices
	1918.			
	30.4.		Work continued on Forward roads under the orders of C.R.E. 49th Division.	
			Battalion located at L.23.b. central, with Transport at L.21.d.5.6.	
			The undermentioned Officers, W.O. and men were awarded honours as shewn for gallantry in action during the heavy fighting and withdrawal on the ST.QUENTIN front in March 1918.	
			Major. G.C. Champion. D.S.O. Capt. J.E.S. Pethick. M.C.,	
			2nd Lieut. J.J. Acton. M.C., Lieut. S.E. Boulton. M.C.	
			No.20581 R.S.M. J.Harrison. M.C., D.C.M.,	
			No.22007 Sergt. W.Twinning. D.C.M.,	
			No.20818 Sergt. H.Sandford. M.M. No.20280 L/C. Milligan A.M. M.M.,	
			No.21043 Pte. W.Seaton. M.M. No.20377 Pte. Prescott J. M.M.,	
			No.21479 Pte. J.Percival. M.M. No.21612 Pte. Jones T. M.M.	
			No.20813 Sgt. J.Taylor. M.M.	
			No.21132 Pte. A.Atherton. M.M.	
			No.20569 Cpl.(L/Sgt) Blake W. M.M., Bar to Military Medal.	
			Strength of Battalion on the 30.4.1918 : 23 Officers. 494 Other Ranks.	
			The casualties incurred during March 1918 as under, and cancel those shewn in War Diary for March 1918 which were not complete as regards verification with the Hospital Sheets the latter not having been received at time of forwarding War Diary. Officers casualties as shewn in last Diary :-	
			Other Ranks. Killed 14. Wounded. 149. Wounded and Missing. 34. Missing. 176.	
			Died of Wounds. 14. Wounded and since rejoined 20.	
			Major G.F. Beal, and 2nd Lieut. A. Hughes have both been struck off the strength of Battn during the month, having been invalided to England in the case of the latter Officer, and	

WAR DIARY
or
INTELLIGENCE SUMMARY.
(Erase heading not required.)

Army Form C. 2118.

Place	Date	Hour	Summary of Events and Information	Remarks and references to Appendices
			Major G.F. Beal unfit to return from leave, and Medical Board ordered by War Office.	
			H. Jenn	
			Lieut. Colonel.	
			Comdg. 11th (S) Bn. S. Lancashire Regt. (Pioneers).	

CONFIDENTIAL.

WAR DIARY

of

11th (S) Bn. South Lancashire Regt.,
(Pioneers).

from

1st MAY, 1918
to
31st MAY, 1918.

VOLUME 32.

Army Form C. 2118.

WAR DIARY
or
INTELLIGENCE SUMMARY.
(Erase heading not required.)

Instructions regarding War Diaries and Intelligence Summaries are contained in F. S. Regs., Part II. and the Staff Manual respectively. Title pages will be prepared in manuscript.

Place	Date	Hour	Summary of Events and Information	Remarks and references to Appendices
L.23.c.9.9. (Sheet 27.)	1918 1.5.		Battalion located at L.23.c.9.9. as shewn in last month's Diary, with Transport at L.21.d.5.6.	
	5.5.		Continued work on forward roads under orders of C.R.E. 49th Division.	
			Changed location on the 5th inst. and moved to new Camp near St.Jan-ter-Biezen.	
	10.5		Work continued on the OUDERLOM SWITCH Line, parties being conveyed to site of work by train	
			Battn. moved by Bus to the LEDERZEELE Area, and located in Billets in vicinity of B.28.a & b (sheet 27) Instructions received that the Battalion was to be broken up, all surplus Officers and Other Ranks over and above an establishment of 10 Officers and 51 O.R.s being disposed of as under:-	
	12.5.18.		301 Other Ranks transferred to the 19th Bn. Lancashire Fusiliers. 300 Other Ranks transferred from the 19th Lancs Fusiliers to this Battn.	
	13.5.18.		38 Other Ranks proceeded with the Battalion Transport, less Offrs Mess Cart, 1 Water Cart, and 1 A.S.C. Supply Wagon, to the 30th Div. Transport Concentration Camp, CUCQ.	
	14.5.18.		381 Other Ranks and 7 Officers (names as under) transferred to the Base Camp, ETAPLES for disposal as reinforcements to other Units.	
			Officers - Captain A.T. Champion. Capt. R.G. Dunthorne. Lieut. W. Bretherton. Lieut. C.H.N. Symon. Lieut. B.F. Mackenzie. 2nd Lt. A.D. Hurley. 2nd Lieut. K.N. Harpur.	
	15.5.18.		Lt.Colonel H.F. Fenn, D.S.O. ordered to proceed to take over Command of the 19th Bn. Lancashire Fusiliers.	
	15.5		The remainder of the Battalion, known now as the Battalion Training Cadre, for an American Battalion, received orders to move on the 15.5.18 to EU Training Area. Proceeded by March route to AUDRICQ there entraining for WOINCOURT Railhead.	

Army Form C. 2118.

WAR DIARY
or
INTELLIGENCE SUMMARY.
(Erase heading not required.)

Instructions regarding War Diaries and Intelligence Summaries are contained in F.S. Regs., Part II. and the Staff Manual respectively. Title pages will be prepared in manuscript.

Place	Date	Hour	Summary of Events and Information	Remarks and references to Appendices
			Bn. Training Cadre, located at BEAUMONT CHATEAU, Nr. EU.	
	19.5		Bn. Training Cadre moved from BEAUMONT CHATEAU, to TOUFFREVILLE, where the 110th Engineer Regt. were billeted.	
	20.5.18.		commenced Training of the Coys and H.Q. 110th Engineer Regt. in Musketry, Gas & P. & B.T.	
	27.5.		Orders received to move Training Staff to ARQOEUVES along with the 110th American Engineer Regt. who were to be employed on the construction of a G.H.Q. Line of Defence in rear of AMIENS Area. 2 Coys per day of the Engineer Regt. at our disposal for Training Purposes, the Staff being divided up in to 2 portions in order to meet the requirements and dispositions of the Coys of American Engineers.	
			On the 28.4.18. Major C.C. Champion. D.S.O. was Invalided to England. Captain J.E.S. Pethick M.C., took over the duties of 2nd in Command on the 14.4.18 the date on which Major C.C. Champion. D.S.O. was admitted to Hospital. Acting Rank of Major given to Captain J.E.S. Pethick M.C. with effect from 29.4.18.	
	3.5.18.		Lieut. W. Bretherton and Lieut. C.H.N. Symon reported to Battn. for duty after a tour of light duty for 6 months in England.	
	9.5.18.		Captain A.T. Champion. and Capt C.J. Dixon M.C. reported to Battn. for duty after a tour of light duty for 6 months in England.	
	11.5.18.		Authority received for Capt. A.T. Champion and Lieut. S.E. Boulton M.C. to wear the badges of the rank of Major and Captain respectively, pending notification in the London Gazette.	
	15.5.18.		Major J.E.S. Pethick M.C. took over Command of the Battn Training Cadre, on Lt. Colonel H.F. Fenn. D.S.O. being ordered to proceed and take over Command of the 19th Bn. Lancashire Fusiliers.	

WAR DIARY
or
INTELLIGENCE SUMMARY.
(Erase heading not required.)

Army Form C. 2118.

Place	Date	Hour	Summary of Events and Information	Remarks and references to Appendices
	18.5.18.		Capt. C.J. Dixon. M.G. and Lieut. H.M. Fieldhouse appointed Divisional Range Officer and Div. P & B.T. Officer respectively, and reported to Div. H.Q. accordingly for duty.	
			On the 20th May, 1918 the following award appeared in Divisional Routine Orders	
			His Majesty the King has been graciously pleased to approve of the grant of the VICTORIA CROSS to No. 20765 CORPORAL J.T. DAVIES, this Battalion, for conspicuous bravery whilst serving in the Expeditionary Force, as set forth below:-	
			For the greatest courage and devotion to duty under heavy rifle and machine gun fire on March 24th 1918, near EPPEVILLE.	
			When his Company on being outflanked on both sides received orders to withdraw this N.C.O. knew that the only line of withdrawal lay through a deep stream lined with a belt of barbed wire and that it was imperative to hold up the enemy as long as possible. He mounted the parapet, fully exposing himself, in order to get a more effective field of fire and kept his Lewis Gun in action to the last, causing the enemy many casualties and checking their advance.	
			By his very great devotion to duty he enabled part of his Coy to get across the river which they otherwise would have been unable to do, thus undoubtedly saving the lives of many of his comrades.	
			When last seen he was still firing his Gun with the enemy close on top of him and was in all probability killed at his Gun.	
			(Authy. XVIII Corps Wire A/68 dated 19.5.18).	
			Information has since been received that Cpl. J.T. Davies is unwounded and a Prisoner of War in Germany.	

J.S. Pethick

Major.

Commanding 11th (S) Bn. S. Lancs Reg. (Pioneers).

www.ingramcontent.com/pod-product-compliance
Lightning Source LLC
Chambersburg PA
CBHW081430160426
43193CB00013B/2239